International Pro

2022

MINGLED VOICES 6 contains the work of sixty-seven poets. The one hundred and thirty-three or so poems were selected from those entered for the International Proverse Poetry Prize in 2021, the sixth such annual international competition administered from Hong Kong.

The International Proverse Poetry Prize was jointly founded in 2016 by Dr Gillian Bickley and Dr Verner Bickley, MBE, in association with the annual international Proverse Prize for unpublished book-length fiction, non-fiction or poetry, submitted in English, which they also founded, in 2008.

Poems could be submitted on any subject or topic, chosen by each poet, or on the subject chosen for 2021 by the Administrators, "Shielding" (interpreted in any way each writer chose). There was a free choice of interpretation, form and style.

Included in the anthology are the poems that won the first, second, and third prizes. Selection to appear in the anthology was also awarded as a prize by the judges. This year, special mention is additionally made of five of these poets.

Poems were submitted from around the world by writers with a variety of previous writing experience.

Brief biographies of all of those whose work is represented in *Mingled Voices 6* are included in the anthology as well as authors' background notes on their work.

MINGLED VOICES 6
INTERNATIONAL PROVERSE POETRY PRIZE
ANTHOLOGY 2021

Poets

Vinita Agrawal, Joy Al-Sofi, Shikha Bansal, Andrew Barker,
Gary Beaumier, Alan Bern, Thea Biesheuvel, Liam Blackford,
María Elena Blanco, Gavin Bourke, Lawrence Bridges,
Lina Buividavičiūtė, Vincent Casaregola, Chan Kwan Ee, Tom,
Margaret Clarke, William Leo Coakley, Audrey Colasanti,
Suzanne Cottrell, Lawdenmarc Decamora, Neil Douglas,
A. Elliott, D. W. Evans, Adele Evershed, Daniela Fischerová,
Casey Hampton, Carrie Hooper, R. J. Keeler, Christos Koukis,
Lynda McKinney Lambert, Susan Lavender,
Birgit Bunzel Linder, J. P. Linstroth,
Iris Litt, Sharon E. Ludan, Wayne Paul Mattingly, Jack Mayer,
Rianka Mohan, Gloria Monteiro, Natalie Nera, Philip Nourse,
Denise O'Hagan, Helen Oliver, Rena Ong, Jun Pan,
Peter Parle, Joanna Radwańska-Williams,
Coolimuttam Neelakandan Rajalakshmi (Raji),
M. Ann Reed, Vinni C. Relwani,
José Manuel Sevilla, Dale Shank,
Allegra Jostad Silberstein,
Hayley Ann Solomon, Abbie Johnson Taylor,
Luisa Ternau, Simon Tham, Edward A. Tiesse, Bibiana Tsang,
Roger Uren, Deepa Vanjani, Peter Coe Verbica,
Kewayne Wadley, Victoria Walvis,
Honghua Wang, George Watt, Michael Witts, Zuo Fei.

Editors

Gillian Bickley · Verner Bickley

Proverse Hong Kong

Mingled Voices 6
International Proverse Poetry Prize Anthology 2021
edited by Gillian Bickley and Verner Bickley.
First published in Hong Kong by Proverse Hong Kong,
28 April 2022.
Paperback edition, ISBN-13: 978-988-8492-48-0
Ebook edition, ISBN-13: 978-988-8492-49-7

Distribution (Hong Kong and worldwide):
The Chinese University of Hong Kong Press,
The Chinese University of Hong Kong,
Shatin, New Territories, Hong Kong SAR.
E-mail: cup-bus@cuhk.edu.hk; Web: www.cup.cuhk.edu.hk
Proverse page: https://cup.cuhk.edu.hk/Proversehk
Distribution (United Kingdom)
Stephen Inman, Worcester, UK
Enquiries to:
Proverse Hong Kong, P.O. Box 259, Tung Chung Post Office,
Tung Chung, Lantau, NT, Hong Kong SAR, China.
E-mail: proverse@netvigator.com;
Web: https://www.proversepublishing.com

Page design by Proverse Hong Kong.
Cover design by Pin-Key Design Co.
Cover image of Hong Kong harbour at night (21 September 2021)
by Gillian Bickley

British Library Cataloguing in Publication Data.
A catalogue record for this book is available
from the British Library.

MINGLED VOICES 6
TABLE OF CONTENTS

POEMS

ACKNOWLEDGEMENTS

All those at Proverse Hong Kong, administrators of the Proverse Poetry Prize (single poems), thank all those who entered for the 2021 competition, and warmly appreciate the helpful and willing participation in the editorial process of those whose poems were selected for this anthology.

We are most grateful, also, for the professionalism and dedication of the judges.

The Hotel Coma, Ordino, Principat d'Andorra, is warmly thanked for its always willing and friendly help with practicalities in the past, which we are sure will resume once travel restrictions make it possible for the judging panel to travel and meet there again.

On this occasion, we give particular thanks to Anne Casey, first-prize winner of the Proverse Poetry Prize 2020, for her opening Message and to Jeff Streeter for his Preface.

NOTE FROM THE EDITORS
and Proverse Poetry Prize Administrators

For this, the sixth annual international Proverse Poetry Prize, poems were invited, either on the entrant's own choice of subject or theme, or on a subject selected by the Proverse Poetry Prize Administrators, "Shielding" (interpreted as each entrant might wish). Any form, style or genre could be used.

Poems were judged by the panel of judges as submitted and the following awards were made:

First Prize
Joanna Radwańska-Williams • 'Confucius Temple in Qufu'
Second Prize
George Watt • 'An Improbable Ruin'
Third Prizes
Maria Elena Blanco • 'Palace Of Winds, Jaipur'
Jack Mayer • 'My Indoor Cat'
Denise O'Hagan • 'In limbo'
Helen Oliver • 'dreamers and dust'

Special mention
Joy Al-Sofi
Lina Buividavičiūtė
M. Anne Reed
Hayley Ann Solomon
Peter Verbica

Several other entered poems were awarded a place in this International Proverse Poetry Prize Anthology 2021, *Mingled Voices 6*.
Their names appear in the Table of Contents as well as on the title page.

Congratulations to all!

Several of the poems in the Anthology were edited by the writers after selection for the Anthology and before publication, but no further judging of the entries was made at this stage.

All writers were invited to contribute a commentary and/or notes on their poems, to be included in this anthology, and have responded in different ways.

Brief biographies of all those whose work is represented in *Mingled Voices 6* can be found towards the back of the anthology.

To the extent that those whose poetry is published here tell us about their occupations and/or working lives, we know that among them (the following description is not exhaustive) are <u>authors and writers</u> (including of biography, ESL (English as a Second Language) materials, fantasy novels, historical romance, non-fiction), editors including of literary magazines, essayists, journalists (including an Op-Ed (Opinion Editorial) writer and a former part-time columnist), literary critics, novelists, playwrights, poets, researchers, screenwriters, translators (including of French, German, Spanish, and poetry), <u>former and retired librarians, teachers and retired teachers </u>at different levels and for different groups in different areas, including American Film, Communications, Composition, Creative Writing, ESL, Fine Art, Humanities, Interpretation, Languages (including English, German, Italian and Romanian), Literature (including American, Bulgarian, English, Italian), piano, poetry, Rhetorical Studies, Linguistics (Slavic and English), Theory of Knowledge, Translation, voice). More than one has worked in <u>publishing </u>for a number of years and a couple have founded their own press; at least one is <u>director of an international poetry festival</u>. <u>Others are, for example</u>, an American Foreign Service Officer, a digital strategist, a retired Australian diplomat, a retired aircraft safety specialist, a homemaker, a retired Principal Inspector of Schools, a couple of doctors in general practice, a farmer, a former attorney, and a former aircraft engineer.

Again, to the extent that those who hold degrees make explicit mention of them (and not all do), we know that among them they hold degrees (including at Bachelor's, Master's and PhD levels) in, among others, American Literature, Anglo-Irish Literature, Computer Science, creative writing, Engineering and Environmental Management, English and Linguistics, English Language and Literature, English Literature, Fine Arts, German and vocal performance, Humanities, Information Studies, interpreting studies, Italian Language, Law, Language and Communication, Lithuanian philology and advertising, Lithuanian literature, Mathematics, Modern Drama Studies, music performance, psychology, philosophy, the Romanian language. One has a DPhil in Social and Cultural Anthropology. One has a Certificate in Poetry. At least one is still undergoing formal education.

One is an Honorman, U.S. Naval Submarine School. "SS" (Submarine Service) qualified. Vietnam Service Medal. Honorable Discharge.

Poems were submitted from Australia, Cap Verde, Chile, the Czech Republic, Hong Kong, India, Ireland, Lithuania, Macau, New Zealand, Singapore, the Peoples' Republic of China, the Philippines, the United Kingdom and the United States of America.

The known or presumed countries of birth of these poets include Australia, Bulgaria, Cuba, the former Czechoslovakia, Germany, Greece, Hong Kong, India, Ireland, Italy, New Zealand, Poland, South Africa, Spain, the Netherlands, the Peoples' Republic of China, the Philippines, Singapore, the United Kingdom and the United States of America.

Some are new or young writers. Others are already well-published as poets, whether in magazines and journals or in book form, some with several published poetry collections of their own. Some are prize-winning writers and/or winners of grants to support their literary work. Several have participated as poets (and in one case as a panel moderator) in national and international poetry festivals and other prestigious events. Some are leaders in that they have formed poetry writing and/or appreciation groups, including online writing communities. At least one is on the advisory board for a literary Prize; one has judged poetry contests.

For about twenty-two of the poets, English is not their mother-tongue. About twenty-seven are men and about thirty-nine are women.

* * *

Entrants were asked to submit their work in English. To qualify, entries needed to be previously unpublished in English, but could have been previously published in another language.

Poems were invited in any genre, form, or style. Nearly all are in free verse; although one poet continues to demonstrate his interest in the figure six – six verses, six lines per verse and six syllables per line – and a small number use specific forms. As identified by the poets themselves, among Lynda McKinney Lambert's poems is an Abecedarian Poem and a poem in Pi format; Thea Biesheuvel contributes a villanelle; and Adele Evershed a "Bop" poem. There are a couple of prose poems. Some use rhyme. Most are in free verse. There are some elegant metaphors (e.g. Peter Verbica's 'Feasting in Mexico').

Again, perhaps most are written in the voice of the writer but some present a persona. (The "back-stories" provided for many of the poems help us to know which are which.) One or two are "found" poems (for example, Anson Wang's 'on the way', recording conversations overheard on a bus journey). One or more are written in response to comments made during a creative writing workshop.

As always, the anthology as a whole displays a wide range of subjects, situations, events, arguments, moods and emotions. The tone ranges from elegiac to analytical, with an occasional touch of humour.

The subject selected by the Proverse Poetry Prize Administrators – "Shielding" (interpreted as each writer might desire) is incorporated in four poem titles, along with the related word, "Shield", appearing in one title. Including titles, the word, "shielding" occurs 14 times in the anthology as a whole. Related words occur as follows: shield (15 times), shielder (1), "shelter" (7) and "sheltering" (1).

Compared with the popularity of the 2020 "set" topic, "Hunger" and related words, this diminished frequency at first suggests a lack of interest. However, several poems focus on or incorporate thoughts about the Covid-19 pandemic, which the set topic, "Shielding" clearly invokes. The words 'pandemic' and 'Covid' occur 15 and 18 times respectively. Some poems describe life during the pandemic. 'Passing Day' seems to describe a day spent observing pandemic protocols. 'A Social Distance' describes some of its manifestations. 'Virus' laments the many Covid deaths in different countries, ending with the poet's description of his own experience during hospitalisation. Another ('Vishvam') refers to the resumed celebration during the pandemic of the Hindu *Khumb Mela*, the world's largest religious gathering, which, as the notes assert, resulted in 300,000 Covid deaths. Other poems use the topic of shielding to explore their inner lives and relationships with others; another focuses on environmental protection.

Poems on self-chosen topics speak of personal experiences – one is a mini-autobiography, a few give insight into the writer's daily life. Some show compassion and careful consideration of people observed on the street, at an airport, on the beach, beginning their day at home, or imagined through the met circumstances of their past. Some focus on mental disorders, family violence, family relationships, parental love and responsibilities, getting to know someone very different from oneself. Some respond to recent local events which attracted international attention – the killing of George Floyd by a policeman in the USA, the murder of Sarah Everard by a policeman in the UK, the mosque shootings in New Zealand, the funeral of the Duke of Edinburgh, husband of Queen Elizabeth the Second. One poet writes about disturbing national events of the past, including the death of Princess Diana and the Hillsborough football tragedy. Another, with her poem about the partition of India in 1947, gives an important reminder that the consequences of such major political events are long-lasting. One poet continues her concern to explore man's place in the environment, his relationship with other creatures, and the chances for survival of all. She also explores what must be of interest to all those who use words – the extent to which they are useful to us and the extent to which they may lead us astray. Related to this, another poet shows concern about the relationship between the digital world and reality.

A handful are intertextual or contain intertextual allusions, referencing or quoting other poems (for example, Keats's 'Ode to A Grecian Urn') For the first time there is a reference to a poem in an earlier *Mingled Voices* anthology. Some are ekphrastic, inspired by other works of art – by a carving, a building, a film, a novel, a painting, a piece of music.

Each poem was judged on its own merits and those selected for this anthology are arranged simply in alphabetical order of poets' surnames and (where more than one poem by a single poet is included) also by title (unless a different sequence was requested by the poet concerned). The poets' commentaries and notes on their poems, requested by the prize administrators during the editing process, are presented as endnotes. The brief biographies of the poets (which were not known to the judges at the time of judging) appear, as supplied by the poets themselves, in alphabetical order of surname.

* * *

All poets have shown considerable commitment to their participation in this anthology. At least a few faced more than usual difficulties in doing so. A handful reported having come down with Covid-19 and at least two were hospitalised.

As last year, we deeply appreciate the consideration and conscientiousness which has been demonstrated and wish everyone, their loved ones and families, a safe outcome from the present pandemic.

Gillian and Verner Bickley
Hong Kong
March 2022

THE INTERNATIONAL
PROVERSE POETRY PRIZE 2022

We very much hope that all who entered for the Proverse Poetry Prize 2021 and all who were awarded a place in *Mingled Voices 6: Proverse Poetry Prize Anthology 2021* will continue to enter their work in future years. We continue to welcome all those who entered for the Prize in 2016, 2017, 2018, 2019, 2020 and 2021 and all who were awarded a place in previous International Proverse Poetry Prize Anthologies in the *Mingled Voices* series. It is a pleasure to recognize as repeat entrants the names of those who have entered before and to compare and contrast their current entry or entries with what we have seen before. We are also always pleased to see new names and we hope that there will be more new entrants in 2022 and beyond.

Receipt of entries for the 2022 competition begins on 7 May 2022 with 30 June 2022 as the deadline.

As in previous years, poets may enter poems either on a subject or theme of their own choice or on the theme suggested by the Administrators for 2022, 'Renewal', interpreted as each poet may wish. Full and updated details will usually be available on the Proverse website, proversepublishing.com.

In the meantime, we hope that those whose poems are included in the 2022 International Proverse Poetry Prize Anthology will enjoy seeing their and others' work and that all their readers will share the pleasure of the judges and the editors in these "Mingled Voices".

Gillian and Verner Bickley
Hong Kong

PREFACE BY JEFF STREETER

The timing of this anthology, *Mingled Voices 6*, edited by Dr
Gillian Bickley and Dr Verner Bickley, is clearly anchored
within the time of pandemic. Indeed, the optional theme of
"Shielding" used in the competition from which these poems
are selected, makes the connection an explicit one. And while
by no means all the poets have written directly or even
indirectly about their experience of Covid-19, it has clearly
shaped the outlook of many of the writers here. Some have
clearly been spending a lot of time at home, others have used
the experience to meditate on their lives or those around them
and indeed upon death. Given the wonderful diversity of
writers involved, this makes up for an intriguing despatch from
the front lines – if, in Shelley's famous phrase, poets are (or
were) the "unacknowledged legislators of the world", then
perhaps these days or at least in this volume they are the non
credentialed journalists of the inner experience of the
pandemic.

Whether that is indeed the case, our poets have often
fallen back on two key themes very common in poetry in
English (especially but not exclusively since the Romantics):
Time and Nature.

The focus on time often comes with a good deal of
sorrow or regret, as that un-Shelley-like poet Philip Larkin
intuited in his poem 'Reference Back'

> Truly, though our element is time,
> We're not suited to the long perspectives
> Open at each instant of our lives.
> They link us to our losses: worse,
> They show us what we have as it once was,
> Blindingly undiminished, just as though
> By acting differently we could have kept it so.

A more modern image of it, but no less uncomfortable, is
supplied in this volume by Daniela Fischerová in 'Protection
Cells':

> Like the doors operated by photocells
> Our days are opening
> They close right behind our backs

The other prominent topic, Nature, although often associated with poems of bucolic ease (going back to Vergil or before in the western tradition), is not without its controversies either. The English essayist and novelist George Orwell complained of getting trolled (in 1930s style) when he dared to mention the subject:

"To put it more precisely, is it politically reprehensible,.... to point out that life is frequently more worth living because of a blackbird's song, a yellow elm tree in October...? There is no doubt that many people think so. I know by experience that a favourable reference to 'Nature' in one of my articles is liable to bring me abusive letters." ('Some thoughts on the common toad'.)

Personally, I'm with Orwell – and am glad that so many of the poets in *Mingled Voices 6* have written about the topic. And, of course, the depredations of industrial society upon the natural world have radically changed the topic, with writers in this volume as in the previous reflecting on the negative influence our species has had on the world around us.

There is so much to celebrate in this edition of *Mingled Voices* that there's hardly the space to do everyone justice, but let's start with the winner of the first prize, the excellent 'Confucius Temple in Qufu' by Joanna Radwańska-Williams. Here, the themes of passage of time and nature are both addressed, as the poet juxtaposes the parallel and independent world/Of nature" with the human one, conjuring up from her memory

> the pigeons
> Over the ruins of Homer's Troy

An economical reminder of not only the indifference of the natural world to even the grandest of human monuments or narratives, but also that other creatures on the planet predate us and may indeed outlive us as species.

Some similar things are happening in George Watts' wryly amusing second prize-winning poem, 'An Improbable Ruin'. In the "jungle greens of every shade and shape" we find some more birds, though they don't sound like pigeons as they "squawk/and screech before cheekily sweeping up/in flashes of red and electric blues." And instead of the ruins of Troy, the poet stumbles over a "rusting leviathan", which turns out to be, in a moment of pure bathos, "a collapsed helter-skelter". At this point the poet moves forward in time, imagining archaeologists "keen for cyphers of sacrifice and sin" poring over the mysterious ruins in some distant future, when the passage of time and the abundance of nature will lend a primitive dignity to the structure it never had while in use at a (20th century?) fairground.

Rather like Watts' archaeologists but probably the less deceived, Jack Mayer's indoor cat is a seeker after truth in nature, as she

> ... stares through windows
> with astrophysical curiosity.

As for many of us who have lived through periods of lockdown in the pandemic years, the poet, taking his cue from the cat, begins to doubt the reality of the world outside and begins to seek

> comfort in the crawl space under my quilt
> on cold nights, when brittle stars
> entice me with their mystery,
> mock my deficient explanations

In the lovely 'Palace Of Winds, Jaipur' by Maria Elena Blanco, we are once again confronted with a ruined structure, but the poet quickly moves us away from the "desolate corridor" or the "fan of stone... supposed to spur a breeze" and directs us to the "rustle of silks" of the

> twenty-seven wives imploring Krishna for
> long life to the maharaja

The switch is from male to female, from bricks to bodies, and from the winds blowing through the structure to the "quickened breath" of the former inhabitants of the palace. The experience she evokes is rather like the one you get walking through the Forbidden City in Beijing, past the monumental, impersonal and terrifying grandeur of the Palace, before finding yourself in a tiny nook that was once the cosy living quarters of the Last Emperor.

It's another switch – in time and also, as in Blanco's poem in scale and focus – that impresses in Denise O'Hagan's moving 'In Limbo'. The poem sweeps us back to a precise, tragic moment 20 years ago – 4.45am – and an equally precise place, as the poet recalls gazing at a

> square of pale blue
> Above the kitchen window

The poem's main mode is metonymy, as it builds its effect gradually through poignant details that achieve moments of unflinching pathos:

> Then,
> I crushed the plastic beaker
> from his hospital tray
>
> In my unforgiving hand; he
> despised
> Coffee in plastic cups.

No glorious triumph over time is achieved by the protagonists, as the poet and her family stay

> adrift in the
> eternal present,
> Scrambling to fill in time and
> compensate our losses,

Yet the beauty of the language allows us, if not a resolution, some kind of respite from the dull ache of remembered pain.

The pain in 'dreamers and dust' by Helen Oliver is altogether different, but no less heartfelt. The poem also takes us back in time via "faint reminders of past lives" also evoked metonymically through "stolid brick edifices" (we're back to structures again) and "colonial statues of famous men" (back to the patriarchy of Blanco's poem). Here, though, the culmination is different, though no less beautifully expressed; after witnessing the despoliation of nature by commercial interests, she leaves the scene, the horrified witness to:

> great sullen dust clouds
> the land's essential life-force dispersing
> blustering east to the Tasman
> shadowing me home

The sibilant /s/ sounds enhance the effect, virtually blowing the dust into our own faces.

Among the poets earning special mentions from the editors, I enjoyed the range in Joy al-Sofi's work, from the menace of 'A walk in the woods' – "it's dangerous out there" – to the calm elegance of 'From an Autumn Hillside' where lovely lines such as

> White puffs drift with the wind
> Far downstream
> Pleasure boats shimmer
> Vanish as in a dream

echo not only classical Chinese poetry but also, somehow, Tennyson's 'The Lady of Shalott' and the T.S. Eliot's 'The Waste Land' - which is quite a feat!

I hope you will also enjoy, as I did, exploring Lina Buividavičiūtė's musing on Haruki Murakami and mental health and M. Anne Reed's own celebration of the wonderful Molly Bloom monologue from Ulysses (an apt tribute in the novel's centenary year) in her poem 'In November's Lenten afternoon darkness'. I am also confident that you will enjoy exploring Hayley Ann Solomon's conjugation of modal verbs and their relationship to the seasons in 'Alchemy'. And I have already come to rely on Peter Verbica for a feast of arresting imagery – literally so in 'Feasting in Mexico' – where, again, time is a key theme, in this case embodied in the poet's own ageing. Nature is once more celebrated, but with commendable succinctness and this time as food:

> in this village,
> we eat everything

I'd also like to commend the powerful, intense poem 'Shielding' by Victoria Walvis and the excellent George Watt's 'Treacle Toffee and the Grammar of Self', which also explores the passing of time and combines a focus on food (rather like the Verbica poem mentioned above) with a meditation on grammar, rather like Hayley Ann Solomon's.

Decades on in my silver years, eyes closed,
the plane's consolatory purr is there now,
still calling me from the leaden mundane.
So I'm here, but there; I'm now and then,
more an adverb of place or time than noun.
With such a singular grammar, can there be
any hope for toffee for me?

I'm sure that whatever your taste in poetry may be, there will
be plenty for you to feast upon in *Mingled Voices 6*.

***Jeff Streeter is Director of the British Council in Hong Kong.
He is writing here in a personal capacity.***

MESSAGE FROM ANNE CASEY

First-prize winner
International Proverse Poetry Prize 2020

A Moment of Pure Human Connection – The Power of Poetry To Transcend Time And Place, To Transform Small Acts of Humanity Into The Essence of Human Experience

My profound and heartfelt thanks to Dr Gillian Bickley and Dr Verner Bickley and the whole team at Proverse Hong Kong for the invaluable work they do to support poetry, and poets and readers like me. It was an exceptional honour and joy to receive first prize in the 2020 International Proverse Poetry Single Poem Prize (following on from receiving third prize in 2019). I have no doubt the current winners and finalists will feel the same sense of enormous encouragement, invigoration and happiness that I felt. There is something immeasurably uplifting, fulfilling and motivating in realising that your work has touched the heart of another person in such a way that you feel they have truly understood and appreciated what you have written. I hope that this year's poets will long enjoy and benefit from that feeling. I heartily congratulate each and every one of them.

What we do as poets is an ancient and potent engagement with the sublime. I like to think of writing poetry as capturing 'sacred moments' in the everyday. The act of writing poetry inspires us to seek out the wonder amongst us, to try and embody the essence and vibrancy of what it means to be alive in that particular moment. Through poetry we have the exceptional privilege of creating an echo in time and space, a resonance that not only evidences our own existence, but which bears witness to our people, our cultures, our mores and our experiences of life in this era.

When we send our poetry out into the world, we cannot know what it will mean to others, where it will find a home. We can only hope that it will reach someone to whom it will have significance, wherever and whenever that small miracle might take place. The power of poetry to transcend time and place never fails to amaze me – its very universality seems to me to be rooted in its ability to transform small acts of humanity into the essence of human experience. It is a constant source of wonder and delight that I can pick up a poem from 8th century B.C. Greece or 7th century Iran or 20th century Chile and feel, *truly feel*, a moment of pure human connection with a poet who has long departed our world. On behalf of poets and readers everywhere, I sincerely thank Gillian and Verner Bickley and their dedicated team for their efforts in preserving so much evidence of our 21st century lives and human experiences through Proverse Hong Kong.

I genuinely feel that one of the greatest gifts poetry offers us is to realise that we are not alone in the world – that our own lives, thoughts and experiences matter and are reflected in others. I also firmly believe that poetry finds its most important place in times of greatest need. The challenges we face currently with the global pandemic of the past two years, the escalating climate crisis and civil unrest across our world sometimes seem to weigh so very heavily. For me, as a poet and as a reader, it is in these times that I turn to poetry to help me to reflect not only on the joy and beauty we can experience in the world around us, but also to remind me of our extraordinary ability, throughout the eons, as human beings to always try to lean into the light. I commend Gillian and Verner and their trusty comrades, and all of the poets in these pages, for raising a lantern in the darkness so that people like me can continue to find human connection, solace and hope through the gift of poetry in our world.

Anne Casey
Sydney, Australia, January 2022

ADVANCE COMMENT BY PAOLA CARONNI

The word "poetry", from the Greek "poiein", means "to make": a poem is something made, and like everything that we create with intention and passion, it requires inspiration, and careful crafting. The final product will be something very personal, unique and irreplaceable.

A poetry anthology is therefore a treasure trove of personal artistic endeavours, working in unison to speak to our souls, and resulting from the act of "creating and crafting". The poems in *Mingled Voices 6* have been written by poets from fifteen different countries. Together, they form a choir with all ranges of voices encompassing different themes: from personal experiences to specific worldly events; from mental health to relationships, and more.

I would like to share my own take on writing for the *Mingled Voices* series, now in its successful sixth year of publication. My previous contributions to this anthology are part of my earlier steps into the poetry territory. Having my work published has been an achievement of personal meaning that gave me the strength to challenge myself and the motivation to continue to write. From those earlier and timid steps, I went on to craft more poems, and eventually, I submitted a manuscript to the Proverse Prize, which turned into my very first poetry collection, *Uncharted Waters*.

Mingled Voices was for me an invaluable springboard – a milestone that gave me the confidence to further pursue and realise my passion. It is an incredible experience to see our own work published in an anthology, to touch the printed page, to read our name, to find ourselves in the company of poets from all over the world, many of whom don't claim English as their first language. What remains, forever, is a testimony to our poetry journey, no matter where we stand now.

The optional theme of "Shielding" for *Mingled Voices 6*, interpreted here in many nuances, is very relevant. In these times, we are constantly shielding ourselves behind masks, taking refuge in our homes, escaping a virus that comes back periodically in all its variants and that confines us in our own restricted physical and mental echo chambers.

Fortunately, words are always a transcendent medium for expressing what we are going through during bleak times.

They allow us to bare our souls and let out our feelings, beyond and "behind the honeycombs of/glass and sandstone" (in the words of María Elena Blanco, 'Palace of Winds, Jaipur', p. 24) of our world – a palace meant to shield us from harm, and from inquisitive looks, but from which we need sometimes to escape to find beauty and to express ourselves through art.

The richness of the themes explored in this anthology and the compelling ways in which they emerge manifest the power of words. Quoting Joy al-Sofi in 'Words' (p. 9) "Do they just connect/Or do they separate?/A bridge always goes both ways." I do believe, as Joy al-Sofi writes, that words can both unite and separate people, but I am certain that poetry can help us come together and heal, as we remove our shields, reimagine a better world, and inspire one another in shared humanity.

The bridge of poetry will always connect those who are looking for shelter, and those who offer a helping hand.

Paola Caronni
Winner of the Proverse Prize 2020
(Hong Kong, February 2022)

ADVANCE COMMENTARY BY CHARLES LOWE

Mingled Voices 6 brings together diverse voices from across the world in an inspiring anthology. 'In Confucius Temple in Qufu,' a poem selected for first prize in the collection, Joanna Radwańska-Williams draws an elegant portrait of the harmony between society and nature in Confucian philosophy, as realized in a temple in Qufu and in the redwoods lining the Muir forest. Andy Barker's 'Youth' expresses an equivalent reverence for history, voicing in his parallel readings of Conrad and Coetzee's 'Youth' an understanding of writing as an open-ended process filled with immeasurable possibilities so long as the craftsperson remains "in awe." Each collected work crystallizes that same child-like pleasure as when the speaker of George Watts' "Unfinished Ruin" comes an incomplete edifice from the past, expressing wonder over its future. I congratulate Gillian and Verner Bickley for their assemblage of *Mingled Voices* 6 – an anthology that, with each hidden gem, sustains the reader with its well-crafted beauty.

Charles Lowe is Associate Dean for Learning, Teaching, and Student Experience, United International College, Zhuhai, China

Face Orogeny[1]

From the small eleven between the eyebrows
to the bunnies on the bridge of the nose,
from crow's feet to nasolabial folds,
lip lines to marionette lines,
the face is a drawing book.

Of all the 648 full moons I've seen so far,
I recall the one that came a month after mother's passing
a gentle smile in the sky
shining through the July clouds
glinting in the rain.

There's a mountain beside me
made of the moss of broken thoughts
that I've culled from the grey mists of my mind.
I didn't know the shade of mountains
could be soft.

I've felt my heart plummet so many times
that I fear it might need braces
to stop from falling altogether.
Something stays locked inside me
like a lift stuck between floors,
like an image in an age-speckled photo
that just won't clear,
no matter how many lines I wear.

Vinita Agrawal

A Walk in the Woods[2]

I stick to the path
Quite narrow at times
All around is beautiful
But everyone knows
It's dangerous out there.

Something unwholesome
Lies in a nearby pond
A perplexing clump
Looking as much like a dead, red rabbit
as anything else that once lived
Except perhaps....
It never did?

The field is reaped, parched
And empty now. Silence reigns
In this space where frogs once
Revelled in the flooded places
Farmers set out green life to grow
In rigid upon rigid row.

Its colours flashing a warning,
Iridescence splendour
In a beetle's body,
Catapults to safety
Ahead of my footsteps.

A reminder this is a jungle
And just who is
The/In danger here.

Joy Al-Sofi

From an Autumn Hillside[3]

1.
September sets forests afire
Flying sparks ride on butterfly wings
Rising mists reveal steep canyon walls
Beside the lonely path rushing waters flow

2.
White puffs drift with the wind
Far downstream
Pleasure boats shimmer
Vanish as in a dream

3.
Beyond the curving hills lies a lake like a mirror
Gathering clouds slow-dance on the wind
They stop overlooking the waters
Seeing themselves they weep

4.
Bird calls fade in the distance
Shadows of soaring rocks
Cast a hush
Across russet fields

Thoughts ignite with passing footsteps
Then fall away to ash
Above, set deep in stone
Words of the poets remain

Joy Al-Sofi

Halfway, Or More[4]

Somewhere between "I'll just take,"
And cooperate
Halfway between chimp and bonobo
The hominids they come…and go.
Except the one we know the best
The only one who's left

How long
Till we too are gone?

(Homo habilis, Homo erectus, Homo rudolfensis, Homo
neanderthalensis, Homo heidelbergensis, Homo naledi, Homo
floresiensis,….)

Joy Al-Sofi

RIP/RAP – A rap in honor of George Floyd*[5]

He was born in Carolina
Brought to Houston when a boy.
As a man he'd had enough
Of that good ole Texas joy.

George Floyd headed north – a fatal course.

His murder shocked the nation.
Played on every media station.
Made our blood curdle
Round the world it hurtled.

Cops s'posed to protect you and me
Save our lives, our liberty.
Showed they're power-hungry punks
Picking on others like bullying drunks.

Sold their souls.
Racists out of control.
I've heard say they're just a symptom
Need to fix the whole damn system.

It's always been too long – too rough
But now that's it, we've had enough.

Make your mind up.
Don't be deterred.
Raise your voice up. Let it be heard.

Starting today, we all say:
"Let this be the last time for police crime.
Make this the final hour of unaccountable power."

Say it again. Shout it louder.
"The last time for police crime!
The final hour of unaccountable power!"

Yeah.

*George Floyd (May he Rest in Peace) murdered on 25 May 2020, by a police officer, Minneapolis, Minnesota, USA..

Joy Al-Sofi

The Perfect Mimic[6]

Leaves lie straight or slant
Along the concrete path
I am startled to see
One leaf
Lift off.

A butterfly soars aloft
Perfectly mimicking
These browning flowering plants.

An evolutionary marvel
A perfect mimic
Unquestioned
We've always thought.

But new discoveries can change all that
They tell a different tale

      (Butterflies and moths
      from 50,000,000 years
      before the advent of flowering plants.)

Fifty million years!
Can't get my head around that.

Just who is the mimic here?

The perfect mimic is
The other way round?

How could we have been/
      be
So wrong?

Joy Al-Sofi

Watching Katmai (On YouTube)[7]

From Hong Kong to Katmai
Without leaving my chair.
Today is the Solstice
I'm watching Alaska
And we're waiting for bears.

Hear the rushing river
See the spill off the cliff
Between me here and
They there
Are a whole lot of
Miles
But there's more than just distance
Between

Us

The internet can disconnect
A compass may point awry
A finely figured map
May have lines drawn
Where rivers are

How can I know
These trees are real
These waters
Swiftly flowing?

I won't feel the stream's
Chill to the bone
Till I swim with the salmon
Home.

Joy Al-Sofi

Word/s[8]

As a child language was in my blood
I cultivated words
Like they were farmed fish.
If one slipped away
I could get it again.
And anyway, there was always another.

In the beginning they were simply a game.
A fun tool to get what I wanted.

Now, I worry about words.

Do they just connect
Or do they separate?
A bridge always goes both ways.

Promising to reveal, words can actively conceal,
Substituting themselves for the real.

A word read is much more than one that is said
And writing even more still.

Could language, our noble guide
Be a traitor,
Nemesis in disguise?

Step by step, word by word,
We walked away from the world.

Our species stepped off the cliff
Into our present free fall.

In the beginning
Was the Word
And now....
In the end
We can no longer live
With/out them.

Joy Al-Sofi

A Trip to the Supermarket[9]

The cool fingers of air draw
well-heeled shoppers in through the doors,
– the hunter-gatherers of old –
to the hallowed aisles adorned with food,
danger replaced with pleasure,
no longer hunting, merely discerning, collecting
produce local and international
nothing's beyond reach
jars of jam, slabs of cheese
sliced pastrami, scented truffles, cured meats.

You can have it all –
the constant refrain of the overreacher,
the hoarder, the glutton, the affluent,
striving, straining, gathering,
until the tables heave under the weight of our longings.

Surfeit bloats the body, the senses feeds,
I become an amalgamation of the sensory
caught like a fly in a spider's web
immovable, helpless, impotent, trapped.
This is *it*, greed is a heavy weight
it slows you down, deadens your gait.

Trapped in the modern cycles of trade,
everything can be bought,
delivered at our doorstep,
we're caught in a maelstrom of want,
the good things, the pretty things,
without them we're a void,
a far cry, a bloated reflection of our lean forebears.

Shikha Bansal

Safe Landing[10]

An airplane in a clear blue
sky gliding without sound,
like a cut-out pasted in a child's
scrapbook, a solo traveller in a desert of blue.

Passengers in cushioned seats
strapped mid-air, clamped
securely to a metal base,
looking out of small, insulated ovals

that blot out the sound and freezing air,
but let the light in so you can see
yourself floating in a sea of cotton,
flushed pink with the setting sun,

a beauty technology helped access.
Featherless, flightless we are lifted
by the thermals with skill only for
plummeting, gravity our only abiding religion,

thinking of the home left behind or
going to, anticipating a destination,
landing gloved and masked,
exchanging one sterile space for another,

the airport for the plane,
waiting in line for tests, then results—
perhaps quarantine or dubious freedom.
Boldness or necessity makes us tear

through inertia, impediments, tests,
or perhaps love or simply survival.
Pleasure trips fall by the wayside
like the hubris of man shattered by a microscopic virus.

> a prayer for safe
> landing
> after a journey of
> forgetting

untempered by
caution,
centuries of claiming
centre stage;
elbowing the sentient to the
edge,
the living off the
planet

the earth keeps us alight
in its gravitational orbit
granting us *permission to land.*

Shikha Bansal

The Wind[11]

Gentle, ferocious; at times a force unstrapped,
it flows without limits, without rules ironclad,
no masters, no chains to tie it down;
it heeds no boundaries, no borders of towns.

Rustling leaves, it gives them a whirl,
wanders through streets, toys with a head of curls,
trifles with skirts, topples hats like kingdoms unguarded,
runs through the streets, chasing those hastily departed.

It rules the sky, ruffles the backs of animals on the hunt,
carries scents in its wake, alerting prey, leaving work undone,
kicking up storms, it forces submission like a demanding
overlord,
shaking, raging over seas, planting tempests and discord.

When it settles for a time, sitting to catch its tired breath,
the living sweat, labour to draw in an air oppressed
in stillness, its magic vanishes like hope in a downturn,
distant troubles draw closer, worries overrun.

In a room I sit, craving its tender touch
to wipe my brow, my troubled furrows,
lift my spirits spent brooding (holding a minor grudge);
I wish for its freedom to roam, to rise above small sorrows.

Shikha Bansal

Youth[12]

—after Conrad and Coetzee—

And, going home for the first time in years,
I saw the folder again.
Frayed cardboard shown through the worn plastic
covering. It was blue. Twenty-one years older than when I first
placed a sheet of paper in it, almost exactly half a lifetime ago.

With the thumb and forefinger of my left hand I
opened it, and as the left side of the folder dropped to the bed,
it took with it about a third of the A4 paper inside.

A4 paper, on which had been written, by someone
pressing so hard that the indentations of each letter, each word,
each sentence, showed clearly on the reverse side of each page
. . .

    poem
    after poem
    after poem.
    In cursive script.

Until twenty-one he couldn't – didn't, write in joined-
up writing.
He had no need to. Desire to.

Couldn't do it because he didn't need to?
Didn't do it because he didn't want to?
I cannot judge for certain now which one of those is
true.

He could earn a man's full wage at seventeen.
Build a house at eighteen.
Employ people at nineteen.
And this is quite easy to do if you can work from eight
in the morning until five at night
    on a windswept scaffold
    or in a waterlogged trench
    on a southern English building site
    at fifteen.

And be thought lucky because he is ahead of everyone
else in the world as he knows it.

Because he earns more money.
More than the teachers who could not teach him at
school
More than every member of his family
More than his friends.
Some of whom are at college.
Who are *so* lazy.
Who say, "What I do doesn't makes me clever than
you."
To which he thinks on what he does each day, each
year and says:
"Doesn't it? What are you actually going to college for
then if not to make yourself clever than me? What do you
actually do all day if *not* things that make you cleverer than
someone who does not do those things?"

And on building sites because he was always the
youngest by far,
while the chancers ran the line,
he built the dog-leg corners,
and the herringbone panels
before he was told to,
to show that he could,
to show he expected the same payment as the best
bricklayers on the site.
Even if they were twenty years older than him.
And he got it.
At twenty years old, he buys his first book.

In my left hand I take the pages in the folder.
My thumb at the bottom I let them fall,
Stopping every ten or so pages to check what's there.
Every sonnet by Shakespeare,
All of *The Wasteland*,
The book: *Thomas Hardy's Shorter Poems*. All of it.
If. Hugh Selwyn Mauberley. Wild Swans at Coole.
And I recite
"All's changed since I, hearing at twilight,
The first time on this shore,
The bell-beat of their wings above my head,"
But cannot bring myself to say,

"Trod with a lighter tread."

It would be affectatious.
And untrue.
And ungrateful to the youth who copied those
hundreds of poems out.
The youth who knew that to give me a chance to exist
The tools he possessed to express his thoughts
Were inadequate to the job.
So he sat at a desk in a heated library from eight in the
morning until five and night
And copied poem after poem after poem to learn to
write.
Until he could construct with ease the essays a
different world would set him.
Until he could write thoughts and ideas, in the time
provided
On whatever he was expected to have thoughts and
ideas about.
And he did.
And he thought, in fear of something missing,
This is so fucking easy, this learning!

Then I saw it.
A poem. A sonnet. A poem he'd tried to construct.
It was not good.
He didn't know how to scan lines, write iambics. He
didn't know that certain words draw attention to themselves
away from the poem and should only be used if you want to
draw attention to the emotions they generate.
The poem was difficult to read. The ink it was written
in had faded. So I took a pen and traced the words in from the
markings he had made on the page,
It ran . . .
"Be close to what you know you do enjoy
And if this passion-call be true for you . . ."
And then, following the indents on the paper I signed it
in the signature I still use. One of block capital letters.

I closed the folder, and with my right hand, placed it
high on a shelf.

And I thought of what he had written, written in such a
way that the indents lasted longer than the ink.
I think that, as he did all that, he knew that I'd be here
In awe of what he did,
Believing I just could not do it now.

Andrew Barker

Panhandler's Lullaby[13]

look away as you glide down the off ramp
pulse the door locks
pray the light to green
or turn up your Brahms

do not glimpse his brief prayer
on tattered cardboard
his three word biography

he will shelter in a vacant doorway this night
mistaken for a pile of rags
suckling on some cheap booze
that will burn a path down his esophagus
while a cutting wind scampers litter past him

yet was he not celebrated at birth
by a mother who sang him back to sleep
after he took from her given breast

there will be thumping music at 3am
that breaks into his unconsciousness
and at some point in the night
the bladder will not hold
and he will shiver and sing out for his mother

come the next evening he will find the old
busker near the underpass by the tent city
and he will blot the dribbled whisky from the scraggle of his
beard
on the back of his sleeve as he wheezes out a cough
and then he will rise unsteadily to toss a few crumpled bills
into the music case
and listen to the trumpet measure sweet notes that echo and
drift off of the concrete

"Play Taps" he will tell the horn player

and his memory will drift back to the war when he watched the
soldier ahead of him

step on a land mine
his body shredded into a pink mist
and he will choose to remember that soldier
even as he wishes to forget

Gary Beaumier

The anger of the frozen, dying[14]

The anger of my frozen, dying friend
is almost impenetrable because
she is now making up long lost time.
What in the world? she asks me again,
not believing she is still alive,
nor that she will die soon. I send her
words and images she can barely
read on her screen. Soon she will have
to hear them spoken: her eyes
go now, her ears may go
last.
I want to read these stories to her.
Please let me, listen to me, I beg her.
She is tiring, and will have none of this,
I cannot understand what you say, she says,
and sends me off again into fog and dusk.

Alan Bern

Avian Villanelle[15]

Birds sitting in the old gum tree
Just doing a retrospective
Snakes in the grass somewhere

They're feathered images of me
my musings less effective
Happy memories somewhere

They don't need to find or see
don't need to be reflective
Mates for them somewhere

Birds sit and wait and see
it wouldn't take a blind detective
Find food for thought somewhere

I know what life demands of me
despite my feathered thoughts I am effective
with unstressed lines somewhere

Sit long enough and we might see
a light, a flash of feathered fancies
there in that mirrored mood a remedy
some food for thought eventually

Thea Biesheuvel

The shielder, the shielded[16]

The shielder is speaking:
"I tower like a bull,
blocking you from all harm.
Against my back, hunched down,
falls a scorching red rain.
My skin is rough and grey.

"That you are the shielded,
so small and pathetic,
I hate and resent you,
but I know what I am.
This is my life's mission,
my joy and agony.

"I cry when I conceive
a life without you there.
I would harden to stone.
Of your minuscule form
I wish I could be free,
but I never will be. "

The shielded is speaking:
"I cower like a calf,
blocked by you from all harm.
Under my face, laid down,
grows a bed of soft grass.
My skin is smooth and pink.

"That you are the shielder,
so big and pathetic,
I hate and resent you,
but I know what I have.
This is my life's mercy,
my fear and ecstasy.

"I cry when I conceive
a life without you there.
I would blaze into ash.
Of your enormous form
I wish I could be free,
but I never will be."

Liam Blackford

Palace Of Winds, Jaipur
(Hawa Mahal, erected 1799) [17]

The so-called palace is a desolate corridor,
a remote wing of the harem, hollow inside,
and outside a pyramidal (male) peacock tail:
a fan of stone drilled with nine-hundred-plus
polychrome windows supposed to spur a breeze.
But the true windstorm was the rustle of silks,
the steps running up ramps of alabaster in
search of a free nook to cry in peace or to
fantasize, recline their forehead or their breast
against the fine sandalwood lattice and confess
their desire to the void – this was the whirlwind:
the twenty-seven wives imploring Krishna for
long life to the maharaja, lest they might have to
become *sati* (pure) from head to toe on the pyre,
vowing eternal love, and lose the privilege of
never lacking Ganges water to remove the *kohl*
from their eyes and from their skin the rosy oxide
dust of Rajasthan. And now the mental blizzard:
to watch themselves draw pleasure and make
themselves seen behind the honeycombs of
glass and sandstone, to see themselves making
themselves seen to her or him, the random passer-
by (instead of watching without being seen), their
lips and nipples surging through the mother-of-
pearl filigree. That was their hour-and-a-half
daily vendetta before heeding another perfect
stranger's summons to the nuptial chamber.

When you admire the façade of the Hawa Mahal
seek not in its niches the stereotyped story
                                        of the wind,
but the eroticised body, the quickened breath.

María Elena Blanco

The Tusk[18]

Not ivory, missing the bright-white
almost tooth-like
luminescent porcelain appearance
and appropriate grain and striations.
Was passed on, bone and synthetic binding,
shaped tusk-like, static, frozen in time.

Dead on arrival,
the chryselephantine sculpture
heavy, in weight like real bone
of those dimensions would be.
The scrimshaw artwork
carved deep into the bone,
etched into the purple-stained blood vessels.

Chinese in origin,
emperors on horseback,
epic, magnificent flowing scenes of Chinese history,
of soaring eminence, erudition, and reverence.
The makers –
artists, prisoners, sailors, kings, queens – who knows?
when there are no initials or signatures,
signs or marks that would reveal the identity of the sculptor,
or sculptors.
Popular in British drawing-rooms
in the late nineteenth century,
in the background of many conversations and writings.

Gavin Bourke

One Of Those Linoleum Days[19]

I'm the street, the flag, the billboard,
the smile, the radio playing mood music.
Today, underneath, behind, above
and around (don't name it) it feels,
studies the mind (don't list). Days arrive
as a surface of aplomb on a troubled week.
No getting used to it. Lurking underground
is the unspeakable – I'll give you a word:
"dashed". Stop. Return to the paved day
where it's easy to live with no thought
fit for a city slicker in a chrome car
top down in nice weather, passing
under banners and blimps and skywriters.
Down under, a readiness to face facts,
and return a broken mind to its golden home.

Lawrence Bridges

Acute psychosis/In the world of Murakami novels[20]
Dedicated for all facing mental disorders

Mist only mist on your eyelashes –
and you feel like living in Murakami novels,
you are in that emptiness –
where no one is able to out-crave anything,
where no one is able to out-hope anything,
no one can out-love anything, where all is
out-lived, merciless merciless land of miracles,
merciless merciless end of the worlds,
you don't discern dreams from reality, perhaps you are that
stuffed wind-up bird, a mechanical cuckoo, having made her
nest on the dial – who will fly above your nest, cuckoo,
who will cover your feathers in tar, cuckoo?

They found you naked in the gateway –
no, you really can't distinguish dreams from reality – mist
only mist on your eyelashes, last night you hunted sheep,
you shot another hunter – he was your father the cuckoo bird.

Lina Buividavičiūtė

Cotard Delusion[21]

I gave you all my blood – it was thicker than water–
I gave you my lungs, liver and kidneys; snakes of my guts
Coil in your abdomen, my hair grows on your head.
Now I am so empty, I hear dead voices in that emptiness –
How sweet is not-to-live – now I am so clean, and my veins
are transparent, nothingness whispers in them –
I dry like a mummy, I preserve my faith, all certain beliefs,
I walk in stalker's zone, in dark streets, spreading silence.
Who can witness my essence, who can confirm I truly
Was in this strange cruelty? Who can give me certificate
Of my birth, when I lie down in melancholia's fog,
When I identify myself as a beautiful fictional bride?
I am starting to forget the name of that movie,
I am starting to run downwind all dust of my previous lives.
No cries, no grip of ten little fingers into this starving world –
Finally, I can say this great triviality –
having emptied the dishes of blood –
having emptied the dishes of time –
having emptied the dishes of obsession –
I can exit this cave of shadows.

Lina Buividavičiūtė

Leda Syndrome[22]

> *So, mastered by the brute blood of the air,*
> *Did she put on his knowledge with his power*
> *Before the indifferent beak could let her drop?*
> —From 'Leda and the Swan', W. B Yeats.

Sometimes I dream strange erotic dreams – I wake up
with the sweat of the womb, nipples erect; misty
stretches, the dregs of consciousness, as if there were
some abnormality, as if everything happened without my will –
I am an incubus's whim, the conduit for bodily energy
on which others feed.

On such nights, I am Leda: white wings clench
my throat, press the cage of my breast; I am conquered
by a foreign power – the spike protruding from feathers –
I am the little wolf of desire, a frail girl, whom none
will offer as recompense for paradise.

The demons who come at night have a gender, and that
can't be desired away by the new ideas of our days.

My greatest fear is to give birth to an idol of beauty,
whose offhandedly seductive gestures will begin new wars.
The quiver is enough, the ecstasy, though unjust in some way,
horrifying, as if the blood of my finger were used
to sign a contract without my will, as if I were condemned
to suffering and pleasure while being a submissive servant, a
dish.

(I am reading a Murakami novel where a man goes to rape
his ex-wife in her sleep.)

Lina Buividavičiūtė

On Devils and Obsessive-Compulsive Disorder[23]

I grew up in a real devil's den – I was told
stories about a girl who was danced to death
by the devil, about a girl who stepped on
a cavalryman's boot and felt the lack of toes.
My grandmother told me that one of our ancestral
homes was built on the bones of witches
who would wail there nights, cackle and laugh;
the lights would dim, and plates would break –
that house is now boarded up. The neighbour saw
a devil turning a grindstone in the field, then found
a fat, knobby finger in the dirt. When I did something bad
in the day, I dreaded the coming train of devils
at night – my first existential fear – and even now
the most horrifying film for me is *The Exorcist*,
essentially about our utter helplessness,
about how austere power can transform you at any time.
When much later, I was alone with my son, fear
of the night left me weak. Scratching at three
in the morning – the hour of the beast – shadows on the ceiling,
I felt the beast was coming for me, coming to possess me.
When I fell under the spell of obsession, my thoughts
became the devil's. I would stare at a knife and think
how I could stab everyone around just like that. I was afraid
the devil would make me behave shamefully – to take off
my pants at a conference, to laugh uncontrollably; I thought,
what if the devil makes me hurt my child? Antipsychotics
exiled the devils to the sixth circle of hell. But I'm still afraid.
I'm very afraid. Of myself and of dancers with hollow shoes.

Lina Buividavičiūtė

Shadows of Mothers[24]

The wide tree boughs of mothers, their dense foliage,
a large shadow thrown, hair the colour of crows,
small glowing daughters within,
inseparable, almost invisible:

such a perfect mother, a teacher, a beauty –
such a coarse, clumsy, ham-fisted child –

stiff dresses, starched collars,
tightly wound braids to the point of pain:

don't stoop, don't smack your lips, don't talk back –

fatal birds, with prim feathers, orbiting
hordes of men, a joke, smashed plates, time
for sleep, my swan, unpretty one, born black.
Your minutes don't matter, all is just moments in time,
posing for family photos, then off to the governess.

It makes no difference what you do: mothers do it better, divide
and conquer, yet you feel so much the archetype with a son,
tucking the frail body into the shade of your crown.

Lina Buividavičiūtė

Stendhal's syndrome[25]

Sometimes, I drown in those stories – it seems
I am caressed by a limitless tenderness,
made real by that which no one could guess,
by what was hidden in that endless palace,
I remember, pregnant, the first months, we
were stuck in Paris, the bankcard was blocked,
and we paid with our last bills, standing in the longest
line to see the Louvre. We naively hoped
to have the melancholy of autumn explained to us,
the quick steps from the assault of darkness,
the time of lengthening shadows where I walked in iambs,
though I thudded up the stairs, no strength left, but there
a wild miracle: the sieves of meaning glowing in the halls –
I scanned them with my eyes, seemingly not even nauseous.

Sometimes, I completely forget to break free of my role,
like when I spend an entire evening looking
at the beautiful bride of death submerged in water.

My child is sleeping, and I "talk about Kevin", overwhelmed,
my breath taken away, having discovered the northern
archipelago,
writing about love without mothers, grinding my teeth, steeped
in nights,
in the menace of days, in reflections of the skiff we row
beneath us.

Lina Buividavičiūtė

XS[26]

dedicated to all who have faced eating disorders

You can't do anything but quietly lie there, suffocating as dust motes
crawl through your mouth, ticks of unlove reside in your bed. On sleepless nights
you would press your eyeballs to the point of pain, making sparks –
 you will not inherit the Kingdom, unable to be freed. Growing pains
in your legs at night: you want to cut them off, to rip out the hair of maturation,
you dream of meat, meat, meat, you dream that you prepare gigantic women for a feast,
their livers protected by gates of lard, and you wake up, your t-shirt besieging
your breasts – too much, too much atomic mass, uncontrollable mass, your belly pressed by your mother, your sister, your grandmother –
their bony hips their bird-like bites their see-through photographs
their size S lives – *You're ugly. You're fat. But you're a nice girl.*
By day you stare at yourself in the glass, a mirror stage without end,
Only you are the judge of the body's trial, you repress your waistline,
you exile your hands, you punish your thighs with no chance of appeal – you divide, divide the cells in order to rule the world – today I'm not hungry, my head hurts, I stuffed myself at school –
the purest pleasure is to dwindle: womanhood withdraws like a crab,
she revokes her blood, and this is your greatest victory,
this is the true veganism of being, unborn, there's not enough iron to kindle
your existence – how wondrous that feeling of disbalance –
you swim and swim above
their bony hips their bird-like bites a girl who can't be made out

in photographs without a loupe. You suffocate, mouth stuffed with a tube,
tied down so you can't pull it out, soft death pouring into you, keeping you
alive, you spit, spit, choke, sixty pounds of victory –
mother sister grandmother – bitches envious of your XS life.

Lina Buividavičiūtė

A Social Distance[27]

Mostly, now, we use social media,
screens filled with faces in boxes
like the old Hollywood Squares,
or a strange form of social prison.

Some carry on in closed offices –
you can hear their murmuring,
from time to time, like the sound
of mice running behind the wainscoting.

Halls, however, remain discretely
silent, except for the occasional
footstep or the distant sound of a door
closing, with the person still unseen.

The break room is empty, yet
the trace remains of someone who
left the microwave uncleaned and
also stole the disinfectant soap.

Sometimes, the lights and vents
are the only voices heard, their
soft-subtle rhythms like hymns
in the dead languages of aging monks.

Vincent Casaregola

The Reptilian[28]

When the Reptilian is born, it is born without skin:
sweet flesh, tender limbs,
the odour of sour milk,
eyes bewildered by the many eyes
reflecting upon theirs: expectant, perfect.

The Reptilian is unconscious, confused
and conditioned in the composition of Things.
It observes the walking chair, the Bing cherry
and the warping tapestry on the wall.
It learns its first word borrowed from the stars
and it has its father's nose and its mother's eyes.
The first time it looks into the mirror,
its life is given Meaning: *It* is given Purpose.

The Reptilian is solitary and cares only for itself:
it flicks its tongue and yearns for attention.
It plots and whispers behind a plate of amour –
scales pointing out to bleed and keep its distance from its own:
there will only be one Reptilian, and one is enough.
The Reptilian is intelligent. The Reptilian anticipates.
It learns to adapt and changes skin to protect its back
from behind; when it spits, it wields the rattle like a sword.

The Reptilian is ephemeral, it realises:
when its mortal body moulds with age, it protests
and falls over a pit of sand in the heat of extremity.
It reminisces then: the *is*, the *was* and what *will* become –
but knowing very well that not a breeze would care.
It climbs into the fridge, recoils, and perishes;
its existence is erased from the bitter soils of the earth
and its corpse remains, abandoned,
desiccated, in the shape of a dry cashew.

Kwan Ee Chan, Tom

A Prayer for my Daughter[29]

In foreign land
My daughter sleeps,
Unaware that her
sedated slumbers
Smooth the years
From her untroubled brow:
A young girl again.
That night I pray
Do not take her from me.

She does not hear
The call to prayer
While gentle hands
Prepare her.
Not alone in anxious vigil:
Turkish families also wait,
"Inshallah" their prayer.
That day we pray
Do not take her from us.

In foreign land
My daughter wakes.
Cocooned in lifelines
Still she lies,
Frail but strong
her old life to reclaim:
Recalled to life.
That night I pray
In thankful joy
At such a Benediction.

Margaret Clarke

The Yew Hedge[30]

You'd think it was simple
To grow a yew hedge.
Arc of dark green
Reassuring and fragrant.
Ambulatory behind
Arch at each side
Beckoning acolyte
To contemplative space.

Mole, badger and muntjac
Watched unseen,
Considered their actions
Lifestyle improvements.

Mole tunnelled
Under delicate roots;
Claiming territory
With guardian hills
Of finest spoil.

Badger nosed a banquet,
Tore up greensward.
Beware those glittering eyes,
Those razor claws.

Muntjac breached green wall,
Forged paths to floral bounty,
Lipped, Oh so delicately
Unsuspecting rose.

Yew struggled, held on,
Grew tall.

Margaret Clarke

Butterfly In The Snow[31]
for Olaf

In the streets of Japan
you wrote your poem of survival,
a butterfly in the snow,
making your socks and flowers
from papers in the trash.

Now in New York, on the black slush,
you have become a bear of endurance
who has learned how to live to the spring.

William Leo Coakley

Complicated[32]

1.

The heart is the river Nile to all its deltas
The heart is an orchestra with four chambers, all in first chair
If listened to, the heart's music would sound of both bliss
And rue. And everything in between. If held in your hand
The heart would turn your skin to a chalice
Your fingers to delicate pincers, as that is
What would be required to hold such a precious thing.

2.

When he died, we found four cases of Jim Beam in his closet
The big bottles. He wore size 13 shoes. All John Wayne
Swagger and tree trunk calves, he was too large of a man
For this petite-sized hole, a mere dimple in the earth
Dug out with a hand trowel in three easy scoops
Our stubborn giant, now a pinch of featherweight dust
Being sprinkled into the soil by a nonchalant nun, her gesture
Routine and blasé, as if adding potting mix to a very tired
planter.

3.

See how the Jack Pine flings its pinecones from its branches
Just throws them out into the sky as if shaking off fleas
Tough love, I say. It's what the fire trees do. They shake
And spit, flick away their children like a tedious remark
Hoping each one will land smack in the mouth of a forest fire
The child born ablaze will be the child that blooms fierce
minded
And kind, humbled by its charcoal beginnings and lick of
flames.

4.

Apparently, Argentinian hospitals had no bed linens back then
Or baby diapers. Expectant mothers had to provide their own
After cutting my umbilical cord they pierced my ears
Hence, the rosa del inca in each lobe. I have been told
I never cried. My mother became so alarmed she took
To vigorous prayer, trying to erase my strange silence
With pious pleading. But I still refused to cry. The world
Was noisy enough, as is. Everything around me, just too loud.

5.

If you have a wooden salad bowl, I recommend
Rubbing it with wood butter to keep it shiny and moist
Alive, some might say. The gesture is also akin to talking
To plants or rubbing a brass lantern to conjure good
Wishes. Your salad bowl is a miracle. Spawned
From a tree with a live, beating heartwood. Show it
Love and who knows what you will glean in return.

Audrey Colasanti

Displaced[33]

They've been pulled off to the side like contraband cargo.
The TSA agent asking, how did you get here?
Who dropped you off?

The little boy is as skinny as a blade of straw.
His ribs, an empty basket.
The father toes a dusty satchel spilling with clothes,
while the grandmother's feet pinch inside a new pair of Payless
shoes.

What it must feel like to be a wren in this world.
Jet-streams overhead, gigantic birds with windows
And silver wings
Gigantic rubber wheels roaring to a sudden stop
below your feet,
The TSA agent asking, how did you get here?
Who dropped you off?

The goat bled like
a frenzied fountain,
blood gushing from its neck,
all that elation and iron
then a puddle of port wine stains in the dirt.
The father, ashamed that he had promised so much.

The grandmother, wincing,
 in her too tight shoes.
Too much pressure, she thinks,
Too much pressure.
Her throat stuck way down at the bottom of her feet

The TSA agent asking
How did you get here?
Who dropped you off?
C'mon, someone, speak
Listen, this is a long way from Ethiopia
I'm just trying to help

Audrey Colasanti

Freeze Frame[34]

The ice on the lake is nine inches **thick. thick** enough for
walking
but I am afraid the ice will **split. split** like a yawning
mirror that has flexed its lips **too wide. so wide**, the ice might
crack
open & eat me **whole. whole** air bubbles slide around
inside **the ice. the ice** that is nine inches thick
frost blooms inside the ice that is nine inches thick. **frost** that
looks like crystal
ferns fanning in a **frozen terrain**. it is beautiful, this **frozen
terrain**
but I am spooked by what is **below me. below me**, a ballroom
floor made entirely of **glass. glass** that could shatter like a cut
goblet, sucking me into its frigid blue wine. even though the ice
is *nine*
inches **thick. thick** as a cement block. **thick** as a railroad beam.
which begs the question: **how thick** is my bravery?
how thin, my fear?
is nine inches the marker between comfort & dread?
why not eight? why not ten?
how thick is that place that nurtures both panic & peace?
how thick are the scars of past ugly moments?
how thick the bandages on a still-healing soul?
the ice that is nine inches thick, it **creaks**
& **groans. groans** like a wounded giant. **creaks** like a tree
branch about to crash **down. down** on my hands & knees
I crawl my way to shore, kicking off my boots in case **I need**
to swim
what is wrong with you? **something** yells. *the ice is nine
inches thick!*

Audrey Colasanti

Gig at the Picnic[35]

Am just a white girl eating an orange
Popsicle, watching a black band
Play that funky music
To a group of all-white faces
Can you stand it?

Look at the white guy trying to dance
All bound up in the pleats of his pants
Master of the cripple step
And the rusty hinge

Look how we try so hard
To clap with vigor after each set
Send our kids to drop bills in the tip jar
While tappin' our feet underneath our seats

Our flip-flops slapping the pavement
But not too loud
It is so obvious
And embarrassing

Dying our hair the color of cherry cola
Inking our arms with tattoos in blues and greens
Peace symbols in purple
The Virgin Mary in shades of glaring gold

Doing everything we can
To prove we are 'more than'
Just white

According to Google, white is not even a color
It is the absence of color
But we don't need Google
To tell us that white is lacking

We aren't all bad
Some of us feel trapped in this vacant skin
It's like gum stuck to the bottom of your shoe
The kind that catches on the sidewalk
Each time you lift your foot

How do you explain the stick of your parents' sins?
The ick that clings
No matter how hard you try to rub it off
With timid claps & exuberant tips

We're just too white
Collar, prude and proper
Too much country club, not enough slum
Too much privilege, not enough pain

Too rigid, too frozen
Too shamed by our ivory past
In other words,
We could use some damn color.

Audrey Colasanti

Meat[36]

She, with her black & blue face
The color of sick licorice
Left eye a weeping cue-ball
Fused shut

Tripped on some rocks, she claimed
While you just sat there
Hunched over your steak
Nose nearly touching the meat

Did we ask, what rocks
Where
Why did we choke on our words
As you sheepishly bit into your steak

We saw the blood oozing
From the steak to the plate
Red as could be
But acted as if you were

An innocent snow-white lily
Incapable of chewing
Up and devouring
The love of your life.

Audrey Colasanti

Oh Mother[37]

head bent down, hips to the kitchen sink
scrubbing your knuckles to shredded wheat
the closed fist of your lips unwilling to speak

oh mother

     oh mother
head bent down, nose to your bible, nearly scraping the ink
ceding to the quicksand that devours the meek

& oh mother, dear mother

head bent down, feeding fabric through the pounding
eye of a needle, the whir of your sewing
machine trying to rev to a roar, or
was it sending an SOS?

because yes, mother

you kept your head bent down
even when father brought out his whipping hand
laying it upon your servile band of too many children

like the satyres en atlante, statues with their heads bent down
perhaps you were navel gazing, seeking answers from the root
of your birth, a roman soldier carved in marble, contemplating
the cosmos through the portal of his belly button

oh mother

     oh mother
head bent down
perhaps all that time you were just counting
your bliss & I with my head bent 'round
misunderstood everything.

Audrey Colasanti

As the Shield Lifted[38]

After a queen bee's maiden mating flight,
she's confined to the hive to lay eggs,
sheltered in place, caring for the colony.
For the past year, the pandemic restricted me.

Protected from weather and disease,
I sat in our house, read, knitted, and wrote
until my body longed for freedom.
Even a homebody needs to get out now and then.

Drawn curtains obscured the sunlight.
Somber mood shuttered our lives,
stifled creativity, and turned
my writing to macabre script.

My spirit needed warmth and freedom.
I gained temporary salvation
from phone calls, texts, e-mails,
and online meeting videos.

Like a newly hatched bee, emerging from its case,
I flew to town, peered through the car window
at masked and unmasked passersby,
but knew I must return home.

I sat on the porch swing,
listened to the chirps of songbirds, crickets, and toads,
and swayed with zinnias and daisies in the summer breeze
while I learned songs and dances of hope.
Nature was my deliverance.

Suzanne Cottrell

Absolute Abyss[39]

Absolute abyss

Bruises the color of sunset
Cascading, careening
Down the side of my face

Each eye
Feathered with blood
Graphic, gory

Hair matted and sweaty
Inconceivable injury

Jagged honeymoon night
Kills kindness

Lunar light lurks and
Murders matrimony

Never again

Obituary for intimacy
Preposterous penance

Qualms never quelled as
Rejected ring falls in the sea

Stranded on an island
Thrown away, tossed

Union unhinged
Vicious violence
Wedding wasted

Extinct emotion
Yesterday forgotten
Zen zeroed

Alecia Dantico

When Manny Pacquiao sprained[40]

the noise jamboree in toda terminals, our regular Sunday
afternoon scared the neighbourhood children for seeing blood

drip from his head, all the force and feeling swam to the floor,
parents cried, and street by arcane street the whole town

buried the fear in its throat, freezing the clock to stop the hurt
of tropical error; that loss was the injured sound of an engine

failing to drive families to church, to a nearby shop after mass.
I've felt my skin fumble when I heard a song from the speaker

of a passing car, a very familiar song I could remember
in the instance of a straight punch combination made possible

by retirement, as winning, according to critics, shouldn't be
compressed on a tiny screen. Whatever that means –

the boxer breaks the mirror of the modern man, comes down
to realize why the future is *un*homed by a heterotopia of hurt.

Lawdenmarc Decamora

Aubade[41]

Like the perfect guest
who knows it's time to leave,
time to rise, get dressed,
to kiss, to hug, to grieve,
to know it's for the best,

to know when love is lost,
to smile at what we had
when the heart is tossed,
and sift the good from bad,
but not deny the cost.

Neil Douglas

Le chat[42]
(after Baudelaire)

In my brain there walks a cat
A cat for all seasons
But when he miaows he's very quiet
I suppose he has his reasons

When he miaows he's very quiet
So tender and discreet
But what he says makes perfect sense
His empathy's complete

What he says makes perfect sense
To me it strikes a chord
He sees me through my darker days
He cheers me when I'm bored

Neil Douglas

Lips[43]

for the cursory brush of other lips,
foreheads, cheeks; lips bitten
　　　　to quiver, tremble to weep.
　　　　Lips open the gateway

to voice with the tongue
as it sticks, slides, clicks on the palate
　　　　to articulate a feast of words —
　　　　peach stone truth, ruby sweet lies,

the sibilant don'ts, the whys,
the because I say so, I say so,
　　　　don't cry, don't cry. I love you,
　　　　hate you,

love you, hate you, love you,
love you, love you. Graze me.
　　　　Kiss me.
　　　　Say me.

Neil Douglas

Mrs Charybdis[44]

With a bucket of salty water
She swirls chalk rainbow from her drive
Waves to sympathetic Scylla
Across the road at one-o-five

What has become of Mr Charybdis?
Who left for Marlins Takeaway
Never brought home her rock and chips
Off the face of the earth they say

Sympathetic Scylla sighs
And tells her rather solemnly
Of sightings down at Elmstead Woods
The Glades in Bromley, Catford, Lee

Scylla smiles and smacks her lips
Life goes on
The bucket drips

Neil Douglas

Sylvia calls Time[45]

for the first time in a long time
the punter wobbles

is washed like a stranded jellyfish
from his stool to the Gents

a gentle splash
on Hush Puppies

a negotiation
with shifting double doors

a stagger to meet with a fish supper
the batter taste of Friday nights

while Sylvia hoover to hand
sucks peanuts off the plush

augurs the weary shuttering
slide of bolts

Neil Douglas

The anatomy of her neck[46]

I dream I am Leonardo Da Vinci,
my genius fingers dusty with red chalk,
considering not her obvious beauty

but the angle of her jaw as I ask her
to extend, further exposing the exquisite
geometry of triangles bordered by her

clavicle, mandible and the taut muscle
I will render faithfully to suggest
the perfect line of force along which it pulls.

Neil Douglas

My house is a superhero[47]

My house is a superhero.
It is the ultimate agent of S.H.I.E.L.D.
The guardian of my personal galaxy.
MARVEL...
What is its mission?
To serve and to keep
To be my constant in change
To be my Metropolis, my bat cave, my lair, my hideout.
WONDER...
What are its powers?
It is super strong.
It can stop the world entering.
It is safe with an infinity lock, designed to keep my most precious possessions from harm.
It is a time traveller – leaving the present behind.
AVENGE...
What are its special weapons?
A cloak of protection that brings solace and solitude.
A safety web that encases and envelopes.
A portal and a window to view other dangerous worlds.
BEWARE...
What is its kryptonite?
The open door
The outside.
Beyond.

A. Elliott

Twineham[48]

I'm a stranger here, one who took the turn
a signpost suggested: towards the 'ancient church'.
A rain bled laminate nailed to a stake slurs information:
Quakers' corner, overgrown, rented gesture, resting place...
Beneath a smear it says no headstones... Non-conformists
harvested in July... afterwards tea, scones, exchanges of
peppercorns.

The Lady with the Evian douses towline phrases,
wipes with a flannel a grey face carved with nouns, verbs,
numbers,
all picked out in black enamel. A trip to Twineham, this lady
tells me,
is incomplete without a look at the lepers' door – the squint:
a grill window proud in studded planks.

It opened (partly, once upon a lack of cure) allowing the
diseased
oblique snatches of a holy show that could, at distance,
magically mend them – although it never did.
No seats, no back row, all-weather witnesses to a Mass
administered to unafflicted worthies, sheltered, warm
(or at least one supposes so) and certainly in need
of lesser blessings than those gawping through a grill.

And yet, at distance, there's inclusivity here: the Quaker dead
cornered for peppercorns, the leper loop holed
sacraments, these,
although centuries apart, remain careful benefits in this little
spot.
Who knows? It all could have been a kindness sold to the
excluded,
something some needed more than most bought it where they
could,
which was here paid into the open palm of off-ledger clergy.

A silver vase slots in the milled hole of her parents' stone
and glints, daring dried grass to dance for it.
　　　　Flowers don't last long here, there's no shade.

Steam lifts off the granite. Her point is made.
The stubby stone casts a pointed shadow: high time defined.
     This place is as it is, she said, peaceful enough,
     and there's no need for flowers now, is there?
The Lady of the Evian moves on; she's not seeking answers
from me.

D. W. Evans

Daisy in Chains[49]

My pale eyes hover above the wrinkled pillow of my cheeks
– nictitating – so I shall not die today
I'm still shackled tacitly to this vulgar time of bedding
Now a day's eye might see the sorrow and stoop –
Remembering how I was told to hide my shiny places
and not speak of tempting sunny day stuff

Pile stones around the hawthorn to stop the cows from coming

I ignored the ladling hands stripping the pale petals
– their spittled symphonies sound in the underground
Because he loves me – he loves me not –
Now they are left to crudle in common necks of the wood –
and we keen to reclaim them by candlelight or leave a trail of
paper doves
 – crying and playing up innocence in fallen feathers
Yet still they say – look closely –
hairs grow in the cracks – even on the loveliest flower

Pile stones around the hawthorn to stop the cows from coming

We should dance like happy hollyhocks in every summer
garden
– as tall as a wish against the violent walls and sermon stones
Then all the flitting things can find sanctuary in our green
towers
We will swish our mighty purple skirts in a flamenco of
tumbling pods
and the seasons will sing – how small it is what we know now
Yet it will be the sweetest story – safely sown by our own
hands

Pile the stones around the hawthorn to save the cows from
coming

Adele Evershed

Protection Spells
(Shielding)[50]

Not even the magic lamp
that you can just brush with your palm
nor the goldfish
fed only with shamrocks and mistletoe since childhood
the talisman, even if it was a gift of love
the letter to Santa Claus
nor the bold mantra of hum
Nothing really helps
Believe me
nothing can protect us

Like the doors operated by photocells
Our days are opening
They close right behind our backs

A handful of bilberries, just picked
Thick cream
And plenty of sugar
That's all life can promise

Daniela Fischerová

A Little Like Love

The lanky girl standing in the sand
opened her arms to the sea
as if preparing to leap

into termini of air or waves,
Everyone else pretended not to notice
how loud the sound of grief can be

when it rears like a wild animal
tooth and claw in feral desperation
to escape this solitary confinement

spilling out past our control
over lips and tongue like fire
racing to devour whatever is near.

And then I wondered if I might be wrong
and she wasn't keening but rejoicing,
for all the pleasures that go unnoticed

passing like shadows under our soles,
there but not there and not ours to hold
like when someone gathers your hand

and doesn't let go or pull away,
as some obligatory kindness
rendered unto the dying or disfigured.

She almost looked like a mermaid,
hair tangled by the offshore flow
spumed foam swept back out to sea.

And as I squinted against the glare
I couldn't help but grin at the sound,
what I perceived as unbridled laughter

competing against ocean roar
in a moment when I felt most alone,
it pummeled my ears and balance

until I filled my lungs with airy brine
and called to the horizon with wild gratitude
for witnessing the intimacy of someone else being.

Casey Hampton

Redshirt Daddy[51]

I watched the show from my father's sofa, distant
galaxies flickered on a cabinet cathode ray tube.

Wagon Train to the Stars
transporters and tractor beams,

my father smoked cigarettes saying
nothing. I pretended to be wanted.

His house, his weekends, his ashtrays
spilled over his reluctant acceptance.

I learned ship names and classifications, men in red shirts
gone and forgotten, unobserved   absences.

I watched Star Trek tuning out father's
snowy reception and hazy living rooms.

When we talk on the phone now, I hear
paternal assumptions like background radiation.

Steady as she goes, I imagine him in a red shirt
while I quietly disremember   his name.

Casey Hampton

Earthly Aliens

Aliens aren't just extraterrestrial beings
Who land in flying saucers.
Sometimes they land in our lives
As fellow earthlings,
Who may seem to come from another planet,
But if we learn their language,
Explore their inner terrain,
And search for common ground,
They will become members
Of our terrestrial family.

Carrie Hooper

Picture Window

I have a magic window
On which I draw pictures
That spring to life
When my heart jumps into them.
I sketch special people,
Portraits of my travels,
Favorite foods,
And nature scenes.
Where is that window?
In the realm of poetry.

Carrie Hooper

Sunrise Traveler

My parents and I
Are driving on Route 220.
No traffic.
Suddenly, a man darts across the highway.
Daddy swerves to avoid a collision.
Who's the man,
And why is he walking on a highway
In the wee hours?
Is he lost or drunk
Or our guardian angel?

Carrie Hooper

Lost Cities[52]

The sunward cities die at night every night.
The city is a body.
The city like a heathen body grows from germ –
  a well chanced out of cliff, or camel tracks, crossed;
  these tides of currency – of hope, water – cities flourish.

But love is just a word unless bent down into ground;
  when hope and water, sun, vanish, a city dies as well.
Then stone and steel offer no defense – clear, thrice-
  dripped water, slow loss of wheat, or calm – shipwreck.
Then, like Mycenae, all future cities vanish loveless.

Always staring in, that peeping-tom sun,
  its red finger writing sky and then the sea.
Was it voluntary that your people fled,
  taken up and gone in early hours? Or cancer,
  that cancer whereof the city's liver's eaten live?

Where are you now, city, where did you go?
Why let the desert sands cover home and well?
Did you fight, or – were overwhelmed?
You left at night, for what, some sleight of matter
upon your infertile busted streets, which remain?

Our Lady of Shalott, cute asphodel, her come-on –
  she weaves by night and day for those that lost
  their sense of self, that didn't keep their spirits high.
Two counts of hopeless – deep bites – kill cities less or more.
The web of life, a tightrope strung thick among two towers.

R. J. Keeler

Maginot Line[53]

"People live down here and there's you gaping at the view"
My love is scolding me
Hallelujah; loneliness has done us in
Ashes is hardness in our lungs; Hallelujah
where are the people, where their fires

My love is a world of no illusions, nature's quadrilateral garment
Male and female elucidation, verbs that arrange significance
Enamel in beauty's mould

The earth's basements boil and islands pour out, my hands take on a feeling
The heart's cables boil and conscience pours out
My blasphemous love doesn't parley with the government
It swarms up summer's pulse, up the mast of truth
My love Jerusalem New York, Hong Kong, Mecca, Poor Suburbs
My love has removed the European locket from its neck

Love and only love is not an invention, man's making
Magnetic storms don't make cockeyed the stars' kisses
My love cannot be threatened
Frigates of birds sound the turning of thought
The bitterness of irrevocable ice and the ransom
for the shores' lost sight

My love shouts that summer's funeral should be at the public expense
It averts the evil eye when bankers dream; This yes, it's social justice!
Your god is smaller than his fame

My love is whatever turns, without cuts, proud and vigorous in the next life
My love is whatever shudders without wearing

It's the chapel where ruined loves kiss each other longingly
The lid of the transparent world, the "no" and the "don't"
My love is the scanning, the approach, the touch, the relentless
rain and shelter
My love assumes responsibility

My love is free speech

Christos Koukis

Ode to Access[54]
A Reformulated E-mail Note to Alice Massa, 2018.

For some reason
I have this problem and
cannot comment on what happened.
I've lost my password!

I cannot access my g-mail account
when I try
to leave a comment.
G-mail is not my friend.

My account says that I am signed-in,
but I cannot get connected.
I have reset the password many times
but can never get into my account.
G-mail is not user-friendly.

I just wanted to say
I read your post on pronouns.
After reading it,
I need to make some coffee.

This problem is undoubtedly
a challenge to deal with
I deserve a blue ribbon for effort.
Gmail does not respond.

Lynda McKinney Lambert

Ancient Texts[55]
(Abecedarian Poem)

Adonai lives in the beginning line
Brings sacred revelations
Composed of words that
Dwell among the holy places
Elohim – psalms reveal messages
From first mark or final brush stroke
Guided by alphabetical order
Hebrew songs of sorrows and praise
Inspired writings – Alpha to Omega
Journeys to bring us together
Kyrios focused on the pilgrimage
Letters form sounds to guide us
Mnemonic reminders of mystics among us
Names of God on our forehead
Omega – It is finished!
Prayers, Hymns, and Psalms
Quietly moving symbols down the page
Respectfully writing my poem with
Successive letters from A to Z
The modern abecedarian is
Usually presented without
Verses and end rhymes
Words shall set us free to dance
X is an artifact of ancient Greek
Yeshua is always with us
Zion. The sacred composition is complete!

Lynda McKinney Lambert

Daily Awakenings[56]

He awakens slowly
shielding his eyes
watching
through half-closed lids,
silently enters the restart
of a typical functioning day.

He splashes in a warm shower
balances a thin torso,
overcautious legs, bony feet
A **virtually undetectable** shiver
moves up his spine
as he speaks of trivialities.

He lies in his safe nest
In a state of anxiety
where everything is in order
gloves, towels, pillows, blankets
doesn't know the day or season.
cognitive decline is irreversible
and incurable.

He lays out vitamins and meds
on the green cotton towel
arranged perfectly to
begins the daily count
"1, 2, 3, 4, 5, 6, 7", he whispers.
Gathers up his defense mechanisms.

On a good day he
picks colorful markers
makes geometric drawings
and calculates more numbers.

Evenings are spent
reclining on his soft bed.
The progression does not happen
All at once.

He views colorful fragments
watches tiny ants, fledging sparrows, traffic,
tree-tops blowing in the summer breeze
shielding the silence
in his world where words
no longer matter.

Lynda McKinney Lambert

Letter to Jack Frost[57]
A Pi Poem

Dear Jack Frost,
First,
I want to say
Thanks
for planning to come
we love to see you arrive each year
but we
don't like you to stay long
just long enough for
ice skating
making snow angels
building round snowmen and women.

You're responsible for bad weather
sinister mischief-maker
coloring the foliage in autumn
freezing cold
frigid
ice, snow, sleet
fern-like patterns on frozen windows.

Old Man Winter
nipping our fingertips
and nose
personification
of wintertime
icicles
dripping down

slippery snow-covered sidewalks
treacherous
sliding
maybe this is not a good time
we can postpone your visit this year

I'd like you to know
Jack Frost
We will welcome you next winter.

Lynda McKinney Lambert

Viewing Red Falls[58]

A response to viewing the installation, "Red Falls," by Akiko Kotani.

Akiko Kotani draws her lines
thick red thread twists and turns,
high voltage shocks of energy

Splurge, plunge, splash, curl.
BEWARE – SCARLET LINES TUMBLING DOWN!
 Criss-crossing, draping, leaping Red Falls

Oh! The color is magnificent!
Gestures of emotion shattering space
standing beside the red waterfall

She holds the red ball of woven images
displaced from towering shadows
near the painted grey ceiling

On rainy summer mornings
she examines the contours of a life-journey
capturing shards of fractured gravity

You are an ancient scribe kneeling
sifting and sorting rubicund threads
harvesting life waiting beneath the surface.

Lynda McKinney Lambert

Warm Thanks[59]

A Reformulated e-mail, to Alice, 12 May 2021

I have been wanting to tell you
thinking of you daily is easy
some time ago, I placed
the lovely shawl which you
knitted for me
on the back of my computer chair.

On some cold nights,
I have put the shawl around me
as I typed on my computer.
Most often, I just enjoy having it
draped over the back of the computer chair
to dress it up a little
to remind me
my writer friend Lynda is with me in
inspiration.

Your gifts of books, poetry, and the shawl
just keep on
giving.

Warm thanks to you!

Lynda McKinney Lambert

The Queen's Staff[60]

I have always walked two steps behind you.
I have always sat beside you.
I was your *"strength and stay"* –
At least that's what you say.

Today, 17th April 2021,
Were you looking for someone,
As, black mask, all dressed in black,
At the chapel door, you hesitated,
You looked back
Before you entered?

Were you looking for me?
Was it me you didn't see?
I still had your back, Lilibet,
There was no need to fret.
I was still there two steps behind you.
Then inside the chapel I sat down beside you.

I've heard them say
It will be cold in May
And also in June
But in the garden my birthday rose will bloom.
You'll see me from your room –
Very soon.

They say my duty's done,
But your duty's not yet done
And will not be for time to come.
Until then you can't succumb.

So my soul still sits beside you.
It still walks two steps behind you.
For my duty's not yet done,
Until together we rest as one.

Susan Lavender

At a Loss During the Time of Corona[61]

The poem you asked me to write,
about nature, creatures, and humanity,
is not forming words or lines,
and even less abides in rhymes.
Alas, barely infected with thought,
only feelings abound, short-lived bubbles in shallow water,
flashes of flying fish in Taipo River.
It is said that feelings are always real –
such as the present fear of the unknown –
but that they are not necessarily true.
Perhaps this we call uncertainty.
Already, science has taken the stage,
dressed in big questions, though shrouded in doubt.
Where we once claimed sovereignty,
we now must profess our quieting.
We know that creatures who inhabit this world
in secret depths and cyclical design,
speak languages of their own.

They bark and buzz and bleat and bay,
they wheek and shriek and whinny and neigh.
They roar and croak and squeak and squawk,
they screech and scream and call and talk.
They dook and hoot and coo and moan,
they grumble and groal and grunt and groan.
They chuckle and laugh and quack and chortle,
they low and nicker and pipe and warble.
They hiss and rattle and honk and howl,
they purr and chirp and snort and snarl.
They gobble and chatter and cry and sing.
They bugle and hum and trumpet and trill.

Only I, the poet, am at a loss for words.
I know, there may well be good in our misfortune,
if we can find it.
It is as though signs were waving in the air,
but we only feel the wind.
It stirs remorse in us, quiet like a field mouse.

It slowly forms a voice that contains
the world and life and humanity,
but forms no words that can be owned.

May this winnowing wind lead us
like ripened knowing leaves
into the soil of humility.

Birgit Bunzel Linder

Virus[62]

I

These crude biers in multiples, in multiples
    The wood piled in cones
        The bricks placed in squares for the recent
deceased
           The   garlands   of   orange-yellow
marigolds
        over the shrouded dead

Their burning in multitudes
    The acrid smells of burning human flesh
    The Hindu prayers

This is not Varanasi and the burning ghats near the Ganges
    This is New Delhi
        There the ambulance workers dressed in blue
personal-   protective equipment
        There the mortuary personnel in their
face masks
        There the dead

II

There aquamarine crosses, there white crosses
    There blue carnation heart arrangements, there yellow
        plastic flower garlands in circles
        There excavating at the red clay in the
hundreds
    Then in the thousands

Saudades de vocês, saudades, muitos saudades

As workers in orange-rubber uniforms and plastic mask guards
    place the caskets
    As they dig the orange clay, wrecking the ground in
        rectangular graves

Parque Taruma with the aquamarine boxes filled with orange clay
Adorned with aquamarine crosses in the thousands
In the thousands
In Manaus
There the dead

III

There the coffins lined the streets
Some in caskets, others wrapped in plastic and cardboard

There the coffins lined the streets, and the dead were put out with the trash
To be picked up, by whom? To be picked up, by whom?
Some in blue plastic tarpaulins

There the dead lined the streets wrapped in plastic and cardboard
And some wrapped in blankets
In Guayaquil
There the dead

IV

The sound of oxygen gas turned on everywhere
Ventilators beeping
Hospital nurses and doctors with N95 masks, double-masks,
And plastic visors and yellow and blue plastic gowns
And eye visors and eye goggles
And scrubs, and plastic hairnets, and blue-plastic shoe covers
Stethoscopes

Doubled-blue-gloves

And a busied hurriedness, a busied nervousness, a busyness
    A determinedness, a determined calm, a busied calm

Patients intubated with ventilators and heart monitoring machines
    And blood pressure monitoring
        And oxygen level monitoring machines
            Patient
cubicles separated with plastic
        curtains

Beeping sounds and oxygen hissing sounds in the ICU

"We must turn the patient over!" "Get him in a proning position!"

    There the dead

V

You have the virus too
    "You", you have the virus
        Even after the first jab of Moderna
        You got the virus

Hard to breathe
    Loss of taste
        Fever
           Aches and pains
    And hard of breathing
        Sleepless nights
          Difficult to breathe
            Breathe, breathe, breathe
            Breathe now
              There the...

J. P. Linstroth

Chia Pet[63]

Water this huge chia pet often and
the grass grows
the trees sprout
the sagebrush wanders
the blossoms unfold.
Don't surround it with space junk.
Don't send your exhaust into its blue.
Just nurture it
and in its barest desert
create oases

and never forget
that if you don't do it any more
you can't return this chia pet
to the store.

Iris Litt

How to Forge a Heart[64]

Do not close your heart to the pain;
there are lessons there – some deep.
Be humble, receive it.

Oh, you may flinch and cry out,
wail and groan, *why me?*

But then you must be brave,
and strong,
and brave again.

Take all the small, raw pains;
forge them in your soul.
Fold them, hammer and
mold them into thin strong
steel against the large pains.

For yes, they may come upon you
suddenly, attack
from an unforeseen direction,
pierce your unguarded heart
that bleeds and bleeds afresh.

And then you will be resolute,
scrape up the residue
and forge ahead.

Burnish your heart
strong, but not hard.

Sharon Ludan

Seeking a Theory of Everything[65]

There may be a clue in the clouds today,
sliding in overlapping layers,
converging, then dispersing,
exchanging secrets
(if only I could decipher!)

Or maybe that lone kestrel
soaring in ever widening circles
is sending a message to mortals marooned below.
But he slips through a cloud before I can catch it.

Thin tops of trees read the curve of the wind,
whispering a hint in a language I've yet to master.

The waves taunt me,
flowers tease;
the hills stand immutable in stony silence.

Still I watch, listen,
while the moon cuts the breakers
with a blissful night sigh.

Sharon Ludan

An Infant's Prologue[66]

Those are my mother's legs spread out behind me –
But they won't let me show you. After
All, this is The Theatre, where we try
Only to convince ourselves, over and over
How brave we are and we are.

I wanted to remain inside, *within*
The liquid world, safe from *air*,
Not splattered with blood, oozing
Battle and thrust forth with my first war
Cry. Born a boy. A baby boy already
Turning towards my mother
Heading for her heart with all my air
Born brawn. But I won't make it.
You can't crawl back in once out.

Wayne Paul Mattingly

Out Of The Shoebox[67]

There he is, my little survivor,
nibbling morsels of me
like a baby Saint.

He seems safe (now)
in the shoebox home
I've prepared him, his swollen
tongue
like a kept promise, mouthing
the bubbled shapes of
sundered words to come.

Everyday, since I found him
convulsing, his tiny feet and
bunched fists
shaking in the air
like some stung thing,
I've filled the void over his
shoebox with my head, repeating
"It's me, it's me, it's me," without one flicker
of recognition.

If I leave lately,
returning to his shoebox sky
I find him making little leaps
and starts as if trying to get
out.

Where would he go, anyway,
outside his shoebox?
Into whose heart? What silence?

His is the blessing
I must hear
before he swallows
his tongue.

It's me, it's me, it's me

Wayne Paul Mattingly

My Indoor Cat[68]

My indoor cat's world is bound
by the walls of my house.
She stares through windows
with astrophysical curiosity
about her unreachable universe.
She studies, with hope eternal, birds at the feeder,
perhaps dreams of escape.
She tests hypotheses, a scientist
probing cabinets for secrets, toys, food,
another perspective from atop the refrigerator,
or pressed against the ceiling
in the crawl space over kitchen cabinets.
She stares at sunbeams, meditates on motes of dust.
The solar system of her senses is her universe.
She is calm. But in the wild, in the predator's shadow,
she would fear death for an instant,
then walk away, none the worse.

I stare through the same windows, at my solar system,
my dot in the universe, and can only conclude
that the hand of God does not extend
beyond my four dimensional keep,
though physicists, our high priests of cosmology,
weave webs of 11 dimensions made entirely of string.

I wonder about stars I cannot reach.
I stalk the shadow of death
(it never leaves my restless probing),
no more successful than my cat in the closet.
I test hypotheses with words and, like her,
seek comfort in the crawl space under my quilt
on cold nights, when brittle stars
entice me with their mystery,
mock my deficient explanations,
like dust motes in shafts of light.

Jack Mayer

Vishvam[69]

India does not need me to speak for her
She has seen pyres before; she will see them again
A long-suffering mother willing to wait for offspring
Who will not fail her

I am trying to write what I feel
But, in trying, I know I will fail
I am a daughter of soil
Struck dumb by fever

The silence of a billion against the shriek of a being
Bent on destruction, bent on survival
A new Duryodhan for a contemporary Kurukshetra
His army gathered on the banks of the Ganges

The river mourns our corpses laden with our multiplicity
As funerals set fire to the night
As a million children scorched by midnight's oil
Bear the burden of our duplicity

I will fail, I know, to speak of this suffering
Too immense for one voice
But a teardrop in an ocean too used to salt
India burns; I simply burn with her

I will fail to tell of who we are, of all we are
Of the dawn of civilisation, of the nonviolent sage
Of a haven for Kipling and Kabir, of the temple at dusk
Ringing its bell in tune with the mosque's adhan
Of a Christian seeking hope in the Ramayana
Of a Sufi saint praising a Sikh gurudwara,
Of the Jain bowing to the Buddhist
And the Buddhist bowing back

The infinite religion that made room for atheism taught me to say
Namaste – the divine in me sees the divine in you
And honours the place in your heart where the entire universe lies

Everything you suffer will come to be within me too
Because karma goes a long way back and we are the same, you
and I

The religion not my own borne of the same soil
Showed me that we have to close our eyes to see far
To see others for who we are

My country is not just for me
It is a notion cradled in everyone's history
To say otherwise is to say something untrue
To say otherwise is to India undo.

Rianka Mohan

I Ask[70]

I ask the bird
that landed
in the noisy branches

the one who flew
And he lost in heaven

I ask
the flowers of the song
Forgotten,
unheard

I ask
The sepals that close
revolted
rigid and become
A magnificent button
lost in safety
of your insecurities

I ask
to the heart
Broken
In two
pieces

one side of the chest
got light
and the other was stone

I ask
the blind letters
I ask
the alphabet of old lights

I ask and ask
If one day
I will be able to protect you

Gloria Monteiro

In the Waking Hours[71]

as insomnia flickers in a broken lamp,
on and off, in frequency of weeping lovers
who hope to see each other in the mixed hospital ward
when the light rises through horizons of
their needs and needlessness of

desires that go down the wrong way, only
today she does not want to smile,
she praises her nurse, she praises her priest,
she praises her absent mother, who had gone
missing many months before

the toddler could say Love is
an illusion, a hangover by the garden wall
of the quivering corridors of blue, the whites become blue
protected, sheltered, covered from the outside
here, in the infirmary of butterflies.

Natalie Nera

The Day[72]

Each dawn awakes, a newborn peace;
Forgotten dreams, forgotten grief;
The day grows old,
I grow less bold;
Then dusk arrives;
My heart, it cries,
But never dies.

Philip Nourse

In limbo[73]

We can circle around the fact of
it
And, like the gulls, swoop and swipe, and
try
In vain to get the measure of it, but when it
happens,
The inevitable yet holds the greater shock.
The phone call
Came at 4.45 a.m.; I looked at
the square of pale blue
Above the kitchen window, and
thought:
The sky will never look the
same.

That it was all over twenty
years ago
Matters not at all; in the
double-take of time,
It could be yesterday that we
drew up outside
Hospital doors yawning their
acceptance
Of people such as us. In
looking down
The deepening corridor of
years, I see
The space he left is still not
emptied, but
Chafes against the string of
incremental actions
And the littleness of life. Today
I make real coffee
Inhale the aroma of jet-black
beans, stretch clingfilm
Tight over tuna and mayo
lunchboxes. Then,
I crushed the plastic beaker
from his hospital tray

In my unforgiving hand; he
despised
Coffee in plastic cups.

On the other side of the world,
a memorial mass
Was said for him, but it is us
who are left behind,
Who are in limbo, adrift in the
eternal present,
Scrambling to fill in time and
compensate our losses,
Chalk up a character for ourselves, and
all the while
Unhad conversations ghost the hall, the
dining table,
With family intimacies that never
happened, for my sons
Only know their grandfather through
hearsay, old photos
And the litmus test of time.

Denise O'Hagan

[nameless][74]

What brought you to that border
your distinction of 'us' and 'them'
so that with such purpose you shot to kill?
How did you choose your targets?
By beard / skin-tone / headscarf ...
I guess, mere presence in that sacred space.

My mother wore headscarves
my sons and brothers have beards
I might by chance have been there –
would you have cared as you slaughtered me
in your hate-filled intensity?

By denying the right of others to exist
you forfeit your own right
to membership in 'our' humanity.

Your 'us' is not mine ...
your 'outgroup' has been embraced
by the people of Aotearoa –
our 'us' includes 'them'.

We unite to subvert your hate
to reject your deadly act –
your so-called manifesto.
Your evil, we repudiate.

Helen Oliver

dreamers and dust[75]
musing on a visit to outback Australia

dried-up drains, sere pastures
serried rows of stunted shrivelling wheat
dusty roads spinning off into the drab flat haze
along this tarseal snake creeping
the hot heavy hours inland

faint reminders of past lives
– Goolagong, Currrajong, Wiradjuri –
interspersed amongst the stolid brick edifices
churches, service clubs, restaurants
colonial statues of famous men
in a rural outback town

no sign of the dreamers
those who were here before
only jacaranda flaunting purple revelry
the dreamtime long ago crowded out, overlaid
by the creeping blanket of farms and mines
and other such commercial pursuits
'... gotta make the land pay ...'

and pay it does, in blood-red soil
now blowing to waste, spiralling upwards
as billowing gales raise great sullen dust clouds
the land's essential life-force dispersing
blustering east to the Tasman
shadowing me home

Helen Oliver

flowers grow from dirt[76]

on the side of a dusty car
"flowers grow from dirt"
– so true

ideas grow from fleeting observations
friendships grow from brief encounters
love grows from hesitant beginnings
and – sometimes – poems grow from sorrow

Helen Oliver

Reflection on Shoes[77]

Think first of Imelda
– one thousand, three thousand?
The actual tally hardly matters.
A passion, a fetish – but beyond that
such opulence
extravagance
pure arrogance in the face of deprivation.

Then contemplate Gandhi
humble
shod in *chappals*
– handmade sandals
in solidarity with the poor
unmoved by status and show
referencing those
low caste and reviled:
the shoemakers.

Helen Oliver

tossed in the tide[78]

like a beach towel left below the tideline
I am tossed and twisted in the roiling surf
tangled in seaweed, draped over driftwood
surged here and there as the tides ebb and flow

will someone find me
see past the mess ... pick off the detritus
mend the scars of loss and grief
see my potential shine anew ...

Helen Oliver

Buried Alive[79]

I like to settle in the living room of my renovated house,
with its white-washed walls and shelves of encouraging books,
lined like soldiers on parade; standing to attention, spines
straight.
Nearby ornaments and photographs chosen and placed on
polished tables.

Throughout the house, the bright coloured doors, shut
and locked, hold stacks of boxes crammed full
of things unspoken. Out of sight, yet still in the mind,
their shadows secreting under them like an overflowing bath.

Looking through laced curtains, I admire my lawn.
Its green blanket, with small Forget-Me-Not flowers tucked at
the edges
like "hospital corners', within a thin layer of soil covers the
deep grave
of bricks and stones the builders left behind.

I might add a wooden shed to keep the tools needed to remove
the stubborn weeds, whose roots always seem to remain and
reproduce new growth, or the hidden stones, turned by worms
in darkness
that pop up at unexpected times, causing me to trip and fall.

Rena Ong

1. Passing days[80]

Nine o'clock

                              avocado with scrambled egg
                              salt, soy milk, decorated by
                              sesame seeds

Nine thirty

                              Zoom meeting

Ten o'clock

                    watering that wanton asparagus setaceus
                    who sprouts like octopuses and seaweeds

Ten o five

                    carrying Bob's rohdea japonica to balcony

Ten fifteen

                              trimming the old snake plant
                    that harbours a stream of small ivory flowers
                              blooming once in a millennium
                              so I heard
                              under the condition of no alleged
                              misdeeds

Ten thirty

                              time to check emails
                              reading like snails

Eleven o'clock

                              meeting on VooV

Twelve o'clock

                              ordering food online
                              Foodpanda or Deliveroo?
                              feeling red, or blue?

Twelve thirty

                              waiting for Deliveroo

Twelve forty

                              waiting for Deliveroo

Twelve forty five

                    becoming impatient with delivery who

One in the
afternoon

                              doorbell playing peekaboo
                              naïve eyes of a kangaroo
                    soaked by avant-garde's spilled soup

One fifteen

                              complaining to Deliveroo

One thirty

Internet broken down …
complaining to Deliveroo

One forty five

plastic box on top of garbage bin
fish bones trying to sleep in

Two o'clock

stopping by Median Inn
asking Duke of Zhou to check in

Three sharp

a dance of
rose tea and roasted pistachios
whose turn to cut in?

Three thirty

Zoom meeting
VooV seminar
Skype interview
…
struggling with forgotten password
costing more than an informatics degree from
Oxford
…
finally, Zoom conference
interpreting services too expensive to afford
…

Nine in the
evening

dry-fried beef rice noodles kissing chilled diet
coke
century eggs feeling eager to marry New York
cheesecake
why bother about the difference between
a smoothie and a shake

Eleven in the
eventide

switching off the starlight
turning on Stacy's favourite movie
– a
love story

Jun Pan

2. Hidden nights

24:00

Meditation Minis

24:30

Sleep with Me

1:00

Stephan King on Audible

1:30

Melody of the Night

1:45

Secret Garden

2:00

need to reply that email from Jena
in a polite manner
despite feeling unhappy about her gardener
...

2:30

Enya

2:45

remember to attend Jimmy's birthday party
his voice is sort of fruity
a ride to the place costs much money
but we can have barbecue at the open balcony
...

3:00

one marshmallow, two marshmallows, three ...
what happened to that pair of bellows

3:15, 4:15,
4:30 ...

is it Thursday or Friday
which bus goes to Causeway Bay
that village girl called Xiao Wei
...
whose gift should I take
his daughter doesn't like chocolate cake
vanilla surely nobody can hate

4:45 ...

one task done, two almost gone, three about to
become none ...

5:00

if I make good use of time
weekend gathering shouldn't be too much a crime

5:30	gosh my words create rhythm!!!

                                                       birds
                                                    chirping
6:00

                                    rays of an orange from the east
                                       through the white sponges
                                                       piercing
6:30

                           blue breeze over emerald stillness
                                          floating sailboats
                                    two silvery cottontails
                flautas with Pinot Grigio light-headedness
7:00

                                                      your face
                                              kept emotionless

Jun Pan

At 3:06 On Saturday[81]

At 3:06 on Saturday, a day like any other,
a nation started getting news, a city began to smother.
A city of warmth, a city of love, a city like no other,
Where everybody knows somebody, or knows somebody's
brother.
Ibrox, Bradford, Hillsborough...will there be another name,
to add to the toll of tragedy and shroud the crown with shame?
...or will this nation finally pay heed to events just passed
with hand-on-heart declare aloud, "Hillsborough's the last".
Oh Liverpool, our Liverpool, your children lived in awe,
They smiled through every hardship, they smiled throughout
the war.
Alas this time, smiles will not be seen,
until the people responsible stand with conscience clean.
At 3:06 on Saturday, a day unlike any other,
a nation jointly mourned, a prayer to the Virgin Mother.
an ever-growing ocean of floral blue and red
was covering the ground that so many have feared to tread.
At 3:06 on Saturday, the Kop sits in a silent mix,
Linked scarves across from Stanley Park, in memory of the 96.

(April 1989)

Peter Parle

Christian's Beat[82]

Tick tick, tock tock, his beating heart is like a clock.
Model fitness pulse is true, balls fly high and passes to.
Tick tick, tock tock, his healthy heart should be a rock.
Solid muscle firm and strong, but nature's cruel and sometimes
wrong.

Playing, passing, curling crosses, he's an artist , pleasing
bosses.
Running, chasing, sliding tackles have his heart held tight in
shackles.
Free to play he is no more, his shattered heart has him on the
floor.
The World stood still and held its breath.
As medics fought to keep him from death.

Pushing pumping, chest gets a thumping, compress 1, 2, 3 & 4
Defibrillator attached and all stood clear, he lay prone upon the
floor.
So, more pushing and more pumping, chest compress 1, 2, 3, 4
& 5.
Defib again is charged to go, hooray hooray thank the Lord,
he's alive.

Peter Parle

Farewell To A Princess[83]

Farewell oh sweet Summer blossom,
Taken early on this wet August day.
Your petals have fallen on foreign soil
Wrenched from the heart of your new bouquet

Your glow gave light to the despairing,
And your presence brought smiles to us all.
Your radiance gave hope to the bewildered,
And your touch made the unworthy feel tall.

There are no more tears left to shed.
Nation upon nation has wept to each other.
You were OUR Princess, but we must not forget,
You are a Daughter, a Sister and a loving Mother.

So our Summer is over, sudden and abrupt,
Visions of long melancholy nights invade,
And the rust of Autumn surrounds our hearts,
But thro' the cold winter the heartaches will fade.

Heaven's needs must be greater than ours
And the gates thereto are high and wide
For you take with you a part of all the people
Who were touched by your warmth and your pride.

Farewell oh sweet Summer blossom
Scotland's thistle and England's rose,
The Daff of Wales, the Orchid of the world.
In the rich soil of Eden, our special flower now grows.

Peter Parle

NOW..............[84]

If you are going to love me,
Love me NOW.............
.....................so I can know,
the sweet and tender feelings
from which true affections flow.
Love me NOW.............
.....................While I am living
don't wait 'til I have gone
to chisel at the marble
sweet words on ice-cold stone.
If you have tender thoughts of me,
Please tell me of them NOW.....
If you wait 'til I am sleeping
With chance to ne'er awaken
Death may come between us
And I shan't hear you then.
So if you love me, just a little,
Tell me NOW, while I still breathe
And I can taste it and feel it and
Happily treasure it NOW...........

Peter Parle

Confucius Temple In Qufu[85]

In the Confucius Temple
I hear the wise birds call.
This cypress grove is as it was
Two thousand years ago.
There is something that the egrets know
And have known for centuries.
They look at people passing by
From lofty nests
In the canopy of Chinese pine trees.
They coexist with the human world,
In the parallel and independent world
Of nature,
Generations and generations of birds
Alongside the seventy-seven generations of the family
Of Confucius,
The oldest genealogical tree on Earth.

The pine trees remind me of Muir Woods
Where California redwoods
Remember pre-Columbian times.
The birds remind me of the pigeons
Over the ruins of Homer's Troy,
Who remember the humans living there
A hundred generations ago:
The voice of Cassandra still echoes.

Confucius' voice rings soft in the temple,
Intermingled with the voices of emperors
Recorded on imperial tablets:
Uphold tradition,
Establish harmony,
Be humble,
Be wise.

The birds look at the human effort to be wise
Continued throughout history.
Nature is effortlessly wise
And knows harmony.

In the sunlight of the May morning
Empty blue eggshells drop from the nests in the trees
As new generations of egrets
Hatch.

Joanna Radwańska-Williams

In Praise Of Imperfection[86]

The chiselled stone.
The diamond's flaw.
The finest thread of silk spun
By the ugliest worm.
We do not need to be
Pure
Gold.
Like the recycling rain, the water of our soul
Slowly
Self-purifies,
The becomes mixed with soil again.

Once, I had one last hate.
She was a teacher who was mean to me; I
Do not remember her name.
She died of cancer. I cried, understanding
She had been mean in face of death
And that she would never come back
To slap my hand with a ruler;
Wishing
That my sole drop of water, love
Had not come too late
To be shared
With her, that we had somehow touched, despite
Our imperfections.

Yet in that drop, reflected, was memory
Of abuse.
Let imperfections stay.
Let them become
A part of who we are. If we cast them out
Leaving no room for hurt or hate
Like distilled water
Then we will never feel the pain
Of contrition
Or the sweet blooming of that mystic flower
The recognition
Of love's return.

Joanna Radwańska-Williams

My Polish Doll Lala Basia[87]

Bash, Barbara, *Basia*, Basha,
Lala Basia was my doll,
Little Barbara, my earliest
childhood companion.

Shura, Alexandra, my Russian great-grandmother,
Babcia Szura, she made
lace dresses and a velvet headband
for little Basia.

Basia was plastic, rosy-cheeked, her nose
slightly indented in some inconsequential brawl,
perhaps my two-year-old temper tantrum
or a fall.

Basia was a redhead, I think.
A cheerful girl.
Her eyes were painted, did not close.
Always wearing a smile.

She was my first doll, an only child
of me, also an only child, until
when I was five, my Mom brought me Bambina
from Italy.

That was a whole story: *Mama*
went to a medical conference in Milan
from Warsaw, ten dollars in her pocket,
succeeded in spending only five

so that with three she could
buy a doll for me
whose real name was Lucia,
but I called her *Bambina*, little child.

Thus my family grew – now I had two
dolls! The richest girl in Warsaw
in 1966. Polish Basia decked out in Russian dress
and dashing black-haired Bambina,

whose eyes closed when I rocked her
to sleep.
What has become of them? I don't know.
Forever they inhabit my memory

playing peacefully, smiling
in a world without tears.
In reality, my grandmother Lidia gave
them away when I grew up

and moved away, to London,
Chapel Hill, Stony Brook, Chicago, Nanjing,
Hong Kong... somewhere along the way
they must have seemed to her unimportant;

she did not ask my opinion. Perhaps
they lived on for another child,
friend of a friend of the family. After all,
dolls are made for children.

Joanna Radwańska-Williams

After The Rain[88]

The drenching downpour,
Of replenishing clouds
Proffered a crystalline sky

The drone of
Happy dragon flies
Sweetened the air

Flowers dangled off
The ornate sprinkles
Presenting its beauty

The day was hopeful
Leaving behind all falsity
As pure as the rain!!

Coolimuttam Neelakandan Rajalakshmi (Raji)

Dream's oceanography

To honor my oceanographer cousin who,
like Neruda, *moves in the university of waves.*
—Pablo Neruda, 'The Sea'

waves crest – phosphoresce silver
in the country of lucid dreaming
where i feel beneath their crescendo
and decrescendo the blue flame breathing –
singing me out to sea –

until then, the sea had been saltwater
wilderness – a terror to be met
protected by insulated diving suits
and life jackets – a challenge to be traversed
by kayaks or ships or desperately swimming bodies –

until then, i had accepted only small risks –
to swim, not Thunder Lake's diameter
but to succumb to its safe circumference –
to discard life jacket – to butterfly stroke

just below surface – to dally among
the dazzle of sun-lit schools of fish, their scales
prisms lighting the green-weeded water-world
with infinitely intersecting rainbows –

the dream awoke me to my blindness –
me, the Scottie dog, lost, alone, paddling
vast metallic waters beneath a vaster
grey sky, asking only, *where's the dock*

oblivious to water's aliveness,
and illness, i had not seen this being;
i had sought the goal, not the Big Dream.
Lucid now, i am one with the dreaming

ocean, the sky, the dreaming swimmer awake,
	the keen doggie's inquisitive nature
celebrating this new silver kinship
	flourishing in waves of grace

ready to protect earth's soul, ocean's soul,
	coral reefs, flora fauna fish until
into all water
	i morph again

M. Ann Reed

Even then, in uncompromising winter[89]

    there is the child, the treasure,
      who, like water, questions

and loves quests.
    A child born of golden proportions,
      like Leonardo de Vinci's fetus in a nutshell,

holding the two whose love had formed him
    while the life force, passing
      through him from the artist and through

the artist to us, inspires that deepest darkness
    where *least ourselves remembering,*
      wholeness finds us.

This child, Luke's hands are ready
    to re-order time and space – cup
      the seven-pound Sandy River stone

(once bedded among stone neighbours
    that know the East Columbia River's oceanic roar
      and the slow tumbling waterfall breaking

into silvery wind-chime
    thirty-second notes beneath
      the fern and moss-covered cliff).

C a R e fully Luke resettles this stone inside
    the brass singing bowl
      and returns to its soul-mate,

the larger dove-grey stone that – *yes* – *belongs*
    inside the smaller brass bowl.
      Tiny hands nest stone within brass,
curve flows with curve . . .
    poetic act invokes communion between
      what had been separated –

stone age from metal age,
  silence from music, emptiness from abundance,
    desire from fulfilment.

Like twin ostrich eggs in sturdy nests,
  the new Still moment glows of inspiration's fire –
    and hums E. E. Cummings' math of meiosis:

one's not half two. It's two are halves of one,
  which halves reintegrating shall occur
    no death or any quantity.

M. Ann Reed

In November's Lenten afternoon darkness, we behold beside the brown paper lunch bag on the well-seasoned, scratched oak table, the wax-paper-wrapped sandwich holding a whole context to be relished twice. He regards, gently, like a gracefully falling, slowly twirling snowflake on a silent night, the neatly folded wrap and then unwraps, fold mindfully by fold, the now rare paper releasing all aromas of her homemade sandwich, feeling her one-of-a-kind touch finger-printing his skin, pausing again before this noon sacrament, as her presence, her face passes over his, as he breathes with her, carefully, once more slicing the turkey, tender avocado crescents, crisp lettuce, arranging – no, playfully patterning them perfectly inside the crusts of her freshly baked wheat bread, spreading the honey mustard for the tang of it. As he savors, prayerfully, each contrasting, complimenting taste growing more pleasure, more gratitude on the tongue, we forget ourselves, lost in his shared dying and living before, remembering ourselves, we inhale our lunches and run to class, leaving him to linger in reverie to re-create with that remaining half sandwich a one-of-a-kind lasting memory. And all during class, the *yes yes yes* celebration of Joyce's Molly Bloom held my focus and all the sandwiches she had made throughout her lifetime – all that gratitude, all that love of life, all that unruly pure playfulness for the flaming joy of it –

M. Ann Reed

Incubating[90]

a prayer for earth turning new,
        wondering how i may serve earth's soul,
                i ask my artist, as E. E. Cummings

once asked his –
        be unto love as rain is unto colour; create
        me gradually – and in a murmur –

a flash – i unfurl rain knocking scarlet
        against red roof tiles – hoofs clopping porous
                upon porous red brick – pink waves
        phosphorescing

through white gulls in flight
        hoping for answering music –
                with lightning's leap, i am one with fire –

a memory of winter keeping the voices
        of roses in the tree rings of my heart –
                i am one with the rush and sway of wind-
        ruffled sea,

holding a tear in the palm of my hand –
        memory of being a snowflake – fragile,
                intricate, melting, dissolving, springing up

a pool of clear water – the fresh deep
        of juniper – the inebriate height of blue
                and then no longer a memory

but the spark of light – the *ting!*
        through finer-than-air crystal.
                i marry that tear with rain – rain knocking

scarlet against red roof tiles – *temenos*
        of snapdragons, roses and wrens –
                in waterfall's plunging steam, i am one

with fire-blown glass, the magic circle drawn
in sand, the warp and woof intersecting
preceding thunder, the still *unravished*

bride of silence and slow time.
i am one with Bridget, bride, bridge between
heaven and earth, dust of earth, dust of stars,

shimmering, shivering, serene, infusing dry
winter branches alive with the rustle of birds –

Who could say nature, wild and unpredictable,
lacks a soul? Who could say Nature does not evolve,
each of us new in every moment?

M. Ann Reed

When someone deeply loves you,[91] *you grow strong;*
When you deeply love someone, you grow courage –

Pondering Lao Tzu's wisdom I climb
Jiangxi Province Plum Blossom Mountain

to Nanjing's famous ancestral tombs walking
the never-smooth path of the faithful friend.

I reflect on who has deeply loved me
and to whom I have been a faithful friend.

Plum trees about to bloom pure white are first
to arrive, even in snow, the faithful friend.

Pearl grey sky, empty of rain, steadfast, attends
flower-stone-music's path of the faithful friend.

Look down. A cross of flower-stone-music marks
heaven and earth meeting the faithful friend.

The stalwart sculpted guardian of Nanjing's
People of Rain-Flower Stones protects the faithful friend.

His watchful silent magnitude penetrates
the entombed – marks him our faithful friend.

Look down. On Xuan Wu Lake's path, at your feet,
sculpted love birds encourage the faithful friend.

Look up. Meet inside his shape from sculpted stone,
the contemplative soul of the faithful friend.

Keeping this *Dia de los Muertos*
(of sorts) on Chinese Lunar New Year Eve,
my consciousness heightens more to meet Paul's
voice suddenly breaking through the grey clouds,

his heightened presence and distinct voice *here*
in my heart and *there* in his presence of the past
filling – enlarging, enriching – the whole

world much emptier until then –

                                    as if
Michelangelo had released from marble
Paul's soul as he had David's – as if Xuan Wu Lake's
Faraday Waves had released his tones.

We remember our dates – walks among primeval
Park Avenue maples – as we now converse
under the red-lantern-lit candelabra-shaped arms
of Nanjing's archangelic plane trees – where we recall

our Friends of Jung chats – our self-questioning
road to integrity – Al Pacino's Shylock
in *Merchant of Venice*, feeling the quality
of mercy raining stronger as we find

each other again. As Milton Erickson wrote
My Voice Will Go With You, Paul's now travels with me –
Paul, my moon river huckleberry friend –
we grow Sunflower strength and courage.

M. Ann Reed

She who watches[92] is three. Is ancient. Ancient as the red-brown, purple-blue cliffs carved by Columbia and Yangtze Rivers. She is who she is when sitting astride her father's shoulders, surveying Nanjing's crosscurrents where ten thousand pedestrian head-tops turn into floating rain-flower stones. Her flowering eyes and their heads weave one river, one dendritic flux through the culture's perplex between Cartesian modernity and classical, always contemporary Deep Ecology. Stilled by nature's first song, she breathes speechless odes lest they be lost forever; she exhales unspeakable praise lest the words become buried in a culture of lies and lost forever. Speaking her new word – *Hua* – meaning language – meaning flower – she refers to the blueprinted flower seeds forming roots beneath the earth joining the underground web of life sensing

on the other side
on a different continent,
from the People of Rain Flower Stones
to the People of Rain, nine-year-old Daphne sitting cross-legged on summer's over-hearing grass to cross-examine her eight-year old Apollo supinely relaxed, the back of his head in her lap: *Are you sure you are in love?* She laughs, cupping his chin, rocking up his head so their upside-down eyes meet as above, so below. Nodding *yes* he lowers his gaze. *Are you sure you are sure you are in love?* She persists, rocking up his head to meet again her eyes. Nodding *yes* he lowers his gaze. *How do you know that you know that you are in love?* She challenges, bringing his eyes up to meet her life-is-round gaze. *Because I am uncertain.*

M. Ann Reed

Mother's Guilt[93]

She carries her guilt like
  a backpack sewn into her skin;
her hopes and aspirations all she holds within.
Who knows what her children will become,
  her fears pounding, louder than a drum,
Ready for young lives to begin.

Feelings of guilt precipitated
  by thoughts that come unbid
of how she let others dictate
the lives of her children; their fate.

That for which she yearns
  – freedom from guilt – she learns
cannot be obtained;
But it can be harnessed, can be reined in,
listened to and wisdom gleaned.

And slowly the tentacles of guilt release their grip
  ever so slightly.
Happiness, contentment, entering
  ever so lightly.

She takes a breath, she sees more clearly,
  all that matters is she loves them dearly!
Doting more when there are ills,
  overlooking all the spills.
The drumbeat's now steady sound,
All this together, together bound.

The guilt is never forgotten,
  its messages heeded, very much needed;
As this guilt guides from within –
  All this that is sewn to her skin.

Vinni Relwani

Partition[94]

A line was drawn
A city split
Fracture formed
It led to rift

Brother and brother
Torn apart
Arms over shoulders
Hurting hearts

Borders now
Where before were none
Sudden danger
Flee; flee, run

Grab your clothes
No, there isn't time
Forget all oaths
Toppled paradigm

Uncles finding nephews
Mothers missing sons
Fathers look for daughters
Families undone

Kidnapped from school
Innocent children
No, too cruel
Compound the sin

Don't look there
Eyes can't un-see
Everywhere
Atrocity

Sarees torn
Shoulders bare
Torture borne
Devil's lair

Heartbreak's wail
Ruptures ears
Beyond the pale
Unvoice fears

Save them please
But no respite
Spare them please
My God, their plight

Get on now
See there, the train
To fate we bow
In the midst of pain

Smoke in my nostrils
Fire singes hair
Too much blood spills
As we leave… *for where?*

Tears pour a river
Through land once our home
Life left behind
Now forced to roam

All that remains
Memories entwined
In the nooks and crannies
Of my mind

Dirt in my shoe
Not just earth, not just sand
That's all that's left
My home, my land

Vinni Relwani

Pandemic

In those days instead of the vaccine they injected me the secret
police.

They ran in my veins during the day,
at night they arrested dozens of cells.
They went around all me,
in empty yellow spaces like Saudi Arabia in my brain
or in the pancreas where the cells collect stamps,
classify minerals and speak like in Waiting for Godot.

In the stomach they secretly filmed
couples of food treated badly by life that revived and
ran hugging and laughing under a sudden shower,
I don't know where the music came from;
or provoked riots in peaceful rallies
manipulating the medium or medium rare meat
like giant termites of the 60s,
the stampede, the screaming, the lost child, the Technicolor;
they spied poets in the games room of the intestines,
pretending to be decadent cells looking for beauty and
alcoholism.

What can I say about me in those days?
With no reason, I goosestepped in the disco, in a lift, in a
funeral;
looking at a miniskirt in the escalator I felt love for the
motherland;
and, needless to say, I had nightmares with giant termites.
My doctor shook his head saying that I should get married.

One day the secret police arrived at a beach where the cells of
my memory were sunbathing with cucumber molecules on
their eyes
and bikinis the size of an atom of helium,
They were frozen and didn't spot the three words in the sky,
majestic, terrible, without indulgence.
When their shadows landed on them it was already too late.

My dear and loyal three words of fire,
No, No and No,

José Manuel Sevilla

You are very special

I was born in a country ruled by patriots.
I grew up staring with awe at the charms of unanimity.
The leaders voted with coordination
such as ballerinas achieve only if starting ballet at four years
old,

not one day later.
Life was like cold soup
but people were like hot tongues,
burnt,
bitten.

We stopped having the future in sight,
we became a society of the blind
although we bought glasses following the fashion,
you didn't even know how the world was going to be when you
          were leaving home
when the only thing you ask for is that someone controls the
          seasons of the year.
Is that a big ask?

I saw girls drawing dicks on the walls and
boys with painted nails
as if that was the most extraordinary thing since the creation of
the giraffe's neck.
One day our city was stuck between two floors.
Light was gone, air was missing. A neighbour I trusted turned
out
to have a magnifying glass inside his head, OMG, how scary,
we went so often together to the restrooms and I didn't even
know
he was hiding a weapon.
Thank heaven, one guy split his skull and promised that we
would move,
up or down I didn't care.

I remembered that once a patriot promised my parents
that he would throw pieces of bread at them from a truck.
And he kept his word.

José Manuel Sevilla

Vagrant Glances[95]

deerstalker cap
opaque visor
white cotton not houndstooth tweed
no one thinks I'm Sherlock Holmes

blue morpho on the shower tile
came from nowhere
a moment later gone
I'm sure I saw it

silver filagree brooch
by the sidewalk
I picked it up
it flew away

towering ancient oak
gnarled limb canopy
I looked up
nothing but a thin flagpole
tattered pennant red and green

visor impedes the vagrant glance
at holes in the sky
they vanish if I look at them
I don't know where they go

Dale Shank

The Valley Oak

The valley oak has weathered many years.
Though next door it towers over my house
becomes a shield against the summer sun.
Its gathering of leaves brings welcome shade.

Next door to me, it towers over my house
huge limbs and small branches curve and bend.
Their gathering of leaves sends welcome shade
as they absorb my carbons from the air.

Huge limbs with small branches curve and bend
leaves glory-green I see with gratitude
as they absorb my carbons from the air
like all the other trees that bless this earth.

This glory-green brings hope and gratitude
the valley oak, my shield and my delight
like all the other trees that bless this earth
and may I ever hear the forest call,

hear valley oak, my shield and my delight.
Each living tree brings gifts to all the world.
May we forever hear the forest call
and answer with a lyric in our hearts.

Each living tree brings gifts to all the world
each one a poem waiting there for us
to answer with song-words within our hearts.
My valley oak speaks graciously to me

words unclear and yet I know it's more
than just a shield against the summer sun. . .
a shield for life to wear as I grow old.
The valley oak has weathered many years.

Allegra Jostad Silberstein

Alchemy[96]

Shield me from winter's bitter bite that I slowly thaw,
warming tentatively where once I was inclined to freeze.

Don't crowd or crush me with bold heat – even a gentle glow
can throw me off kilter,
so slow am I to trust.
Don't speak to me of hope filled 'may' – when all I need,
needs 'must.'

'May' or 'might' is spring,
bright hope flinging its buds this way and that,
begging for something to root.
But 'must' is something deeper,
the dell of winter creeping into crevices and
staying, against all odds, with a stubbornness
that is admirable.

If you stand steady and fast, ready to shelter me from the worst
of winds with a patience I cannot fault, you might halt my slow
progression to frost.

I am lost in your gaze, so ablaze with your certainty that I feel
not a thaw but a transition,
not more of what I've known, but something heady in itself.

If this is true, you are an alchemist.
Perhaps, through stealth, you've enticed the wealth of my ice to
melt into myself,
shedding lead for flame and flame for fire, doubt for truth and
truth,
desire.

Hayley Solomon

Shadow-thought shielding[97]

I think in shadow-thoughts, grey monotones shifting in fleeting
flashes
of insight.

Beyond the brightness of bold certainties lie the little flickers
that lick, the tiny flames of confusion confounding my
principles –
and with that, my certainties.

It takes bravery to face them head on
and I am not that brave, only aware that somewhere,
somewhere in that head of mine,
there is a spectrum that weighs truth and justice, wrong and
right,
motive, incentive, hope and fear and
sometimes finds me wanting.

For those times my thoughts shield me from myself,
lest I despair, or worse, discourage the very disclosures so vital
to my humanity.

I see them, for they linger long in the shadows,
filtered and fitted with undertones of silver,
liquid mercury of soul.

Because they are subtle, shadowed, shielding…
I find I can tolerate the presence of these thoughts
And rely on their
impassive constancy.

My shield of shadow-thoughts
strengthens,
without breaking.

Hayley Solomon

Silence, a shield[98]

Is it self-indulgent for me,
a relative stranger, to say I know your pain?

No, I can never know it, but I can conceptualise it,
and it seems harder than most pains to bear.

Even empathy is disallowed, for
In allowing empathy,
one tacitly acknowledges there is cause –
and acknowledging anything, anything at all,
Is strictly forbidden.

Perhaps it is best to stay silent –
reticence may be the greater gift,
but hard to give.
Yet silence is at once absolute and uninterested.
It is neither disinterest nor uninterest I
feel, so that too, seems wrong.

Perhaps if I skirt around inflammatory words –
The words of the watchful,
Words we take for granted
but should not,
ever –
Perhaps *then* I might share something of my heart
without unthinkingly jeopardizing you and yours?

If you are in pain, if you are watching a cancer spread
all around you, helpless to help and unblinking in shock,
If through an abundance of caution you cannot cry, cannot ask
for excision
And can only lie
helplessly,
I am with you.

You wear your silence as a shield and so, I fear, you should.
Mine,
my avoidance of words, my singular lack of the language
of expression, will be your gift, wrong though it might seem
and bitter though it might be.
I hope the darkness recedes. I hope for hope.

Hayley Solomon

The Girl with the Flaxen Hair[99]

With fine, golden curls gleaming in summer sunlight,
gazing eyes, long lashes,
cherry lips so tempting to kiss,
she stands on grass, silent.

As my father struggles to play, on the piano,
the flowing melody and harmony
that Debussy so beautifully created to depict her,
the girl with flaxen hair
dies a slow, tortuous death,
every wrong note, every pause
a stab to her heart,
until she crumples to the soft grass.

Oblivious, Dad continues
to plod through the piece,
note and chord by painstaking note and chord
until he brings it to a discordant conclusion.

Abbie Johnson Taylor

We, Flowers on Roadside Verges[100]

We, flowers on roadside verges
who smile at passers-by,
mowers may axe us
any day, at any point.
Our only shield the falling rain,
while the mowers cannot work.
Weeds, as they say, only good
to be cut and disappear,
our hues and our buds
nothing in their eyes.

Yet, we will grow again,
with our colours and our scents;
we, who contemplate the sky,
who dream in the moonlight,
who drink of the rain
and love any terrain;
we, who are not ashamed
to look up and shine our beauty
in their eyes,
before we are trampled upon
and the bees come back to find
just cut grass....

If only the mowers would stop and could think,
our scents would make their dreams soar;
they would rush to catch them in the air
and we would all be free again

Luisa Ternau

Sheltered in their Worlds[101]

Two seniors take shelter on a rainy morning;
Near strangers who greet each other in passing
Each morning as they take their daily stroll,
Preventing age and memory take their toll.

"So I heard you're a poet," he started chatting.
"Not at all, I just write jingles for children."
"And what do you do?" the other enquired politely.
"Oh, I am interested in, and teach, Religion and History."

"Poeta Nascitur, non fit," he continued in Latin.
"Hardly, hardly, I simply put words into a pattern."
"I am in awe of those who can really write poetry."
"I am even more in awe of someone so scholarly."

And so in that downpour under the leaky awning,
They shared their beliefs, their experiences, their longings.
One a true scholar, a learned sage, a devout steward;
And the other, who simply loved to fiddle with words.

Simon Tham
26 June 2021

Ha Noi Alley[102]

The odors
of heated exhaust from scooters and cars,
sewage, ladies' perfume, grilling meat, tropical fruit and
hanging poultry
merge and embrace
the narrow, crowded walkway.

A short-haired young mother
spoon-feeds her child its first solid food
as the grandmother shouts encouragement and praise
her cries of joy punctuated with hands clapping.

Further on
spit-roasted dogs are stacked in small mounds
on waist-high metal counters
as if they were an offering to a frowning deity.

Next door
in the far corner incense burns and its smoke wanders
among the flowers and gifts at the ancestors' shrine.
On a thread-bare sofa a young man and woman kiss and caress
each other silently
their breathing ghost-like
not wanting to draw attention
from card-playing parents or departed grandparents.

Across the way
two boys watch cartoons on a flickering small screen TV
the volume turned low, their laughter muffled as they become
super heroes
and play-fight with worn pillows.

The voices
from the homes hover in the alley and are dampened
in the cloudy humidity
the sounds of unnoticed lives
on the cobbled stones.

Edward Tiesse

Yellow Paint in My Blue Room[103]
after Vincent van Gogh's *The Bedroom*

Yellow paint in my, Blues.
My, Blue Room.

Yellow smudge of acrylic.
On the window, in the sky.
On this wall of, Blues.

Yellow yellow yellow yellow yellow yellow yellow yellow
yellow yellow yellow yellow yellow yellow the sky, yellow the
ocean, yellow the night, yellow my shadow trapped in grey and
blue.

Yellow
Yellow
Yellow
Bright –
Beautiful
Yellow

Rain
Yellow
Paint,

Yellow this day away

Bibiana Tsang

The Shielded World in Restaurants[104]

Restaurants provide a great shield always
From the boredom and tensions of ordinary days.
The human body requires food to stay alive,
But restaurants help our depressed psyche revive.
For many years I have enjoyed dining
In restaurants famous, ordinary and declining.
In Bombay I ate tandoori chicken and naan
In a restaurant that was like a little barn
Where a girl always sang Stranger on the Shore,
And I felt shielded from every war.

Evening meals in restaurants
Seem like journeys to another world,
For all the daily stress and chores
Which can be worse than repetitive bores
Suddenly disappear and vanish
As one's taste buds take one from dish to dish,
And one forgets the usual daily mess
When worries go from boredom to distress.

I have dined in restaurants everywhere,
In Taipei, Hong Kong, Beijing, Tokyo and near Time Square
Only just to name a few.
No matter where, the restaurant takes you
To another well-protected world,
Where you are shielded from everything fate has hurled.
The cuisine delivers a lot of pleasure,
But the environment allows one to enjoy the leisure
Of feeling free as one enjoys the food
In a decorative place that makes a very happy mood.
All those dinners so many years ago
Leave lovely memories that never go.

Roger Uren

It Had Begun Then...[105]

That space in the wall still waited,
no one had discovered
only i knew the spot
where i had loosened a brick.
Your steps nymph like,
your movements poised,
you glided across the stage
i watched you from that magical space
i had created in the wall,
quietly loosening a brick one day,
reminded of a balistraria,
who's the archer, though, i chuckled.
i had watched you every day, day after day –
afternoons shadowed.
One day you left
it was your grande jeté
my only dream was you
i went my way too
to return years later
to my space in the wall
my wrinkled eyes peering
at your nimble-footed pirouette.

Deepa Vanjani

Child[106]

Sober this morning,

looking at the
silent mouths
of over-turned bottles.

There's an ashtray
filled with smudges
and smoked-over notions.

I rise to take a shower.

Naked, I have no pockets
to hold my words.

A cascade of chill
before I feed the cat,
take a long drive,

and bury a child.

Peter Verbica

Feasting in Mexico[107]

Everything here is being eaten:

the armadillos,
the mountain chickens,
the stingrays,
the locusts
the brightly-colored Toucans,

even the months themselves
yellowing in calendars.

We filet each day
out of gold-filled watches,

as if it were a skeleton
lifted with a fork and knife
from cooked fish.

Stand on your head
for a moment
and walk on your hands.

You'll spot the sun
hung in the sky,

and between blinks
mine diamonds in the dewdrops.

The paradox is that the young

hover like hummingbirds
and sip rather than gulp
from the nectar of life.

(Their afternoons seem to last forever.)

I am among the older now,
having just passed 60.

Even my cigars don't seem to last,
as I puff on the balcony
of this Spanish colonial.

I see the dogs dancing in the yard
and my grandchildren at play.

Dinner will be arriving shortly,

and in this village,
we eat everything:

insects, wild honey, pets
and, especially as we age,

like *un grupo de coyotes*
con trajes marrones,

our past, our present, our future.

Peter Verbica

Secret Garden[108]

In the morning mist
rising from the runway,

the plane's ceiling feels lower.

Perhaps it's just the day's
first light.

We're waiting for fuel,

and the bubbles
from a child crying
to stop

their effervescence.

My hands smell
from an alcohol towelette
which I've opened carefully,

like a prisoner of war
with a letter from home.

The paper inside the foil
is wet and cool and thin.

I am half asleep,
going through the checklist.

I think, for some reason,
of a litany of things
I've seen,

the images working
their way like foxes
through a winter forest.

I'm almost embarrassed
to share them with you:

a kangaroo drowning
a dog in a river,

a dead cameraman
bull-rushed by a hippopotamus,

does lining up to mate
with snow monkeys,

luminescent green algae
growing on the backs
of alligators,

a line of school children
wearing black masks

waiting to enter a museum
full of dinosaur bones,

a corridor of combination locks
suspended in the center
of doors,

tilting a wing to make out
a dirt strip at night,

the runway illuminated
by safari vehicles' headlights.

But hats off
to the creativity
of my oldest brother
just after he retired

on a postal pension.

He donated the rest
of his savings
to a children's charity,

just so he could have dinner
with its elegant spokeswoman.

(He swore that it was worth
every penny.)

"I'm not what people think I am,
you know," he said she said.

"The funny hats,
the one-of-a-kind dresses,
or estate jewelry,"

she continued,
her recognizable voice
beckoning,
inflecting,
hypnotizing
listeners for three generations.

My brother set up a tent in
the loft of our barn
after "The Last Supper,"

with her as he called it.

He reminded me of an owl
seeking shelter in the rafters.

I would discover him
at various places on the ranch:

sweeping dust
into hay chutes,

sitting in a wicker chair
chewing tobacco,

pouring a bowl
of milk for the kittens,

pulling a calf
out of a cow,

refitting a box
into a spring,

stretching wire on a fence
with a ratchet.

After a few drinks,
at the end of a long, narrow table
he would repeat this, his favorite story.

"Her hand ... it was like
holding a hummingbird,"

he explained,
cupping the air.

"And her eyes like dark diamonds,"

as if he were reaching to
touch frosted grapes.

I would wait for him to finish,
and hope, for him,
that he wouldn't choke up.

"She got so quiet
when she spoke of eating
tulip bulbs with her family –

so they could survive
during the war."

During these reminisces,
you could catch him in a slow smile
and decades would disappear
from his face.

"We live a lifetime,
but there are only so many
of *those* moments,"

he would insist.

"To be in the presence
of a dragon opening its eye,

or the passing shadow
of a comet's tail."

His eyes would well
for the predictable finale:

"For such a woman
to allow you
to follow her footfalls
and show you her secret garden ..."

Peter Verbica

The Runts[109]

We live in a cross-eyed world,
full of those who still throw virgins into volcanoes
and expect it to rain.

Forgive them for blaming
disease, pestilence,
and other minor frustrations on their chosen one

rather than study their own unshaven faces
and bloodshot eyes in broken mirrors,

rather than admit their specific, modest velocities
vis-à-vis the awe of an ever-expanding universe.

In the midst of this madness,
I have been asked to take care of the runts,
the drunks, the gangsters, the addicts,
the addled and the whores.

They come to my oaken doors,
not in single file but as a mob
and beat upon it with their naked fists
like Martin Luther
upon the carvings of saints,

as if they are the first to tear down
the statues and crosses
steal the silver,

split marble heads and arms
into powder and grit,

as if they are the first to abandon
their babies to the wild,
or have their skin sluff
with the leprosy of ignorance,
bang upon their shields with swords,
or plow salt into the fields.

Above us, the whine of a jet engine
and a contrail,
as I watch the crowd pillage their city,
shit in their beds and wooden bowls,
topple their own history,
loot their own library.

They've succeeded in bringing down the cathedral,
in torching the temple, the synagogue,
the monastery and the mosque,
struck down these outdated spires
which once stretched their fingertips towards God.

Take some comfort
from the wind which carries away
the smoke of burning hides.

Know that though I have been beaten and stripped
and shamed from town,

I know that all is not lost.

Yes, they've burned the painting by Goya
of Saturn eating his son.
Pried gold from the molars of the dead.
Devoured their own horses in retreat.

But, there's good news to be had.
I am still alive with a satchel of seed:

To save the underdogs.
To lower a rope to those thrown in the well.
To save the runts.

Peter Verbica

This Snow[110]

Ulrich, would you believe me
if I told you what I discovered,

like a wandering star buried
in the engraving of an educator?

Europeans have been busy
for decades
and I've watched them from afar,

residents of the old cities and villages
in particular,

as if they were a flock of birds
to observe with a pair of binoculars
and a rainproof notebook.

I've seen what they do to their history,
busy taking putty knives
full of modernism,

mudding over
the past's beautifully
hand-crafted walls.

You rascal! You're no different!

It all came to me
when I bought the etching
of a President with six fingers;

he holds a magnifying glass
and eyeballs his stamp collection.

The jealousy we have towards
the genius of the past:

the sweeping folds in
the stone lap of a weeping mother,

the philosophers who speak
to our souls while we are sleeping,

paintings which mark
each intersection of Western Civilization.

Before you blitzkrieg over the past,
let me share with you
a few scraps from the pages
which didn't burn.

There are more clues
if we're patient enough to look for them.

I will mail you more letters
with my explanations.

The wrong waterfall in the Philippines.
The bulldogger painting of Ben instead of Bill.

You keep arguing the importance
of the present,

but every generation does.

I'm unconvinced
that all our touchstones should be cast
into the sea.

Thank the prolific Pole
who hid the names
of his friends and family
on a balcony and a stairway.

With each discovery
of his whimsy,
our humanity is reinforced.

Our genetic matrix
holds fast against the void.

(Take the time to read
the Morse code along the
perforated edges.

I've sent these to you all
the way from New Zealand.)

You've been frantically searching
for an empty room.

Remove your Bauhaus watch
and set it on the dresser.

Those survivors from the past
have some important
clues for you.

There's more to find in the postcard
which I sent.

Zeppelins are fine, but
imagine the thrill
of flying in an inverted Jenny.

Here's what I found once
we landed in an open field
and I removed my goggles.

It's the imperfections which
we cherish years later,
despite our quest for perfection.

You've been in search of
an empty room.

Come, my friend.

Let us open the doors to
our own lost culture,
for a whole library awaits us.

We are like cattle in a Western Storm
and the trail which takes us home
is worth remembering,
especially in today's whiteout.

Especially in this snow.

Peter Verbica

Eggs & Toast[111]

Let's go somewhere that's adept
At forgetting.
The taste of breakfast,
Your name as crisp as the edges
Of toast.
Sun-bleached & silent.
The front door closed tight.
Let's go somewhere far,
The awning left pure & untouched.
I woke up & you were the first thing
On my mind.
I grabbed & held you tight,
Leaving before the sun rose too high.
Digging my fork into a plate
Of eggs.
The shifting of salt then pepper,
The illusion that there's more than
What's really there.
Do you know of a place like this?
I'd really like to go.
It doesn't matter where, long as it's far
& you're there with me.
Let's run away as adults & pretend
That we're kids.
Up all night, unable to sleep.
A feeling that constantly feels
Fleeting.
I woke up & you were the first thing
On my mind.
Your name drenched & soaked
In the middle of my mouth.
Flaked & savored.
A feeling that constantly feels
Like it's fleeting.
You taste great with jelly.
The way you spread so little of yourself
& make it seem like a lot.

It's some feelings you never
forget.
No matter where you are,
Not all toast & eggs taste the same.
No matter how much fun you're
having.

Kewayne Wadley

Freely[112]

There are over a million things
To do in the name of pleasure.
Over a million more that involve
Company.
The person I could be,
The person I'd love to be,
Over a million things that could go wrong.
This thought a wave pattern found
In an ocean of sheets,
The shore of the mattress bare.
The meeting of my fingers interlocked
With yours,
The earth rotates & bends sideways.
Without hesitation we are poured
Up down left & right,
Over a million things that could go wrong.
Lost at sea in complete darkness
I cling to you to keep warm.
Lost in the earth, you blush morning.
Shedding light to infinity.
Your face a cathedral of a million things
That could go right.
Smushed & paused in excitement.
Finally.
A religion that doesn't require
A curriculum.
The earth rotates & bends,
I am baptized in the liquid from
Your lips & like a fish I am alive,
& like a fish I can breathe without fear
That you'd be stolen & renamed.
Robbed of over a million things
That could go right,
Between the sheets we hide.
I cling to you to keep warm, lost in the earth
You blush morning.
Shedding light to infinity.
Finally.

A religion that doesn't require
A curriculum.
The person I could be,
The person I'd love to be,
Without fear.
I wander you freely

Kewayne Wadley

Sunburnt[113]

She sprawled out across the sky, bored,
Perfectly sun-kissed.
From a distance she could fit
In my hands.
Day, the name we hold dearest
Day, the name of the memory I placed
her above all else.
I too, lay sprawled out, beneath her.
The intensity of how she makes me
feel,
A region I know well, sweltered &
swollen,
Without walls or halls to contain the
effect she has on me.
She took my hand & gave me the gift of
her presence.
My heart but a burning bush from this
intense percussion, this rapid sensation spreading steadily,
rapidly.
A giant in my eyes.
I've climbed the highest building &
collapsed beneath her.
Black & wilted,
I am the wick without promise of
tomorrow

Kewayne Wadley

Shielding[114]

*"If Nature abhors the void, the mind abhors what is
meaningless. Show a person an ink-blot, and he will start at
once to organise it into a hierarchy of shapes, tentacles,
wheels, masks, a dance of figures."*
—Arthur Koestler, *The Ghost in the Machine*

Shielding is currently paused.
    the advice to shield has ended

Who has been **shielding** and why?
What does **shielding** mean?

      clinically extremely vulnerable people
      stay at home

             Electromagnetic **shielding**
             the process of lowering...

        vulnerable people
         burial

shielding definition is – something that shields

a device or screen
that protects
against harm
        -ful...
        vulnerable
        people defined on medical grounds

How to use **shielding** in a sentence

How long will **shielding** last?
Will **shielding** be
          extended?

What is **'shielding'**?
                 shielding and
                    being shielded

little research has examined
perspectives on coping

little research has examined

shielding advice
to help people make
informed decisions

SHIELDING. meaning
noun [U] (STAYING AT HOME)

a method of protecting
yourself
staying at home and having little
guidance

if you are identified as clinically extremely
vulnerable

you are no longer advised
you should continue to...

You should continue.

Shielding materials are being produced from patented high-
tech...

find out more
who it applies to
what to do
if you're a shielder

...by eliminating external influences due to,

Galvanic interference
Capacitive coupling
Inductive interference
but you can
Wave

...by minimising ALL interaction

between those who are
extremely vulnerable

solutions are provided
you cannot go
into the workplace
we explain – what this means

for people with heart

with
a single shield

public, private
noise

enclosures, barriers
permeability

pull, repulsion
balance

high risk of severe

for people with heart

means a barrier around

or within

that helps

conceal

the light

Victoria Walvis

All the time[115]

Cloud White and Sky Blue
stick to each other like glue.
However, Blue knows not
White's affliction and affection.

Blue thinks maybe I can
change into Eagle Brown's shape.
Or maybe Brown can fly
a little high
enough for me
to caress his wings.

Let there be wind
so that I can drift further away.
Maybe I can find
Brown's traces on the way.

Let there be rain
so that Brown may stand,
looking up.
And I am right there waiting.

However, White knows not
Brown flying up
is to search for preys downwards
rather than looking upwards.

Wind rests
Rain relaxes.
Blue is still
with White.

Anson Honghua Wang

On the way[116]

Journey time: 15 minutes
(one female passenger in a phone call)
You suffer from tiredness.
He suffers from aches.
There is nothing we can do about this.
I did not have breakfast.

Journey time: 20 minutes
(The male minibus driver shouting)
That kindergarten,
you never paid before.
Even though you are holding the kid,
this is the rule you cannot ignore.
since he obviously goes to kindergarten.

(one female passenger standing up awkwardly)

(The minibus driver shouting)
I am not talking about you.

(Another female passenger responding)
I always pay although my boy is less than three.
He is so tall that I would not let him take minibus for free.

(The minibus driver shouting)
I had only one seat available.
I told you not to get on.
You are so unbelievable.
Now I am overloading.

Journey time: 10 minutes
(one female passenger in a phone call)
Two weeks of medicine.
Just wait and check the condition.
That same female physician.
That same room twenty-one.
She need to spend that long on one patient?
Almost 20 minutes,
for just one?
I did not cook.

Anson Honghua Wang

An Improbable Ruin[117]

Cramped jungle greens of every shade and shape.
A part-worn path tells of others passing,
but very few, for rank weeds are willing.
Arrows give directions but a smart wag
has turned them about to face each other,
so he too is likely lost. Where are we?
Could be anywhere. Exotic birds squawk
and screech before cheekily sweeping up
in flashes of red and electric blues
to tall trees far above, shade from the sun.

It's all tropically predictable –
noble trees, hanging vines, dense undergrowth –
until the large unexpected clearing
where a spiralling vine-covered ruin
coils in and out of the thick jungle wall,
a steel serpent, rusting leviathan,
that has seemingly lost its head and tail.
It's really a collapsed helter-skelter
out of place, the nearest town far away
and that a poor topological blot.

Try to hear erstwhile screams of joy or fear,
but you will not get behind the bird song
or the cacophonic cicadas' hum.
Or try to search for other fun-fair wrecks,
such as rusting bumper cars, ghost-train rails,
or shattered mirror maze. Seek as you may
there's nothing else to find. Yet, I like to think
ages hence, archaeologists will come,
keen for cyphers of sacrifice and sin.
Because of this desire they will find them,

marvelling when the solstice sun peers through
the crestfallen coils to a magic spot.
"How wise these primitives were!" they'd sigh.
"What great god demanded such an icon?"

They'll search for meaning in the cuneiform
written across a former sign exhumed,
garish hues and risible hey-ho runes
reappearing a little at a time,
through the patient touch of a soft brush,
and peevish puffs from an aerosol can.

George Watt

Poor Oot[118]

From the Glasgow poems: 1958

Gingerly into the huge black Princess
with its leather scents, taking care not to
jab my leg with the end of the kilt pin,
or flash underwear we're not supposed to wear,
tightly grasping bags of coins saved for months.
My pig smashed: pennies round enough to fill
a palm; thruppence with heavy castle gates.
My place by the window: a dickie seat,
folding down at the touch of a button,
the other seats plump and fixed for grownups.

Children on the pavement raring to go.
"Poor oot! Poor oot!" they chant – their right, their due.
Faces pale, knees knobbly, woolly jumpers
darned again with different colours of threads
smelling of mold or damp or last night's chips.
The engine turns, almost without a sound,
edging away from the granite curb. "Now!
Windows down!" A rain of coins on scramblers
forgetting skint knees, sprained wrists, jabs to eyes.
Rewards lie in wait for their newfound wealth:

Fry's Cream Bars, Spangles, Love Hearts, Acid Drops
or toys from Japan – wherever that is.
Dispensing thus, I could have been a prince
off to Shangri La or Aberdeen. Pure joy?
No. As we drove down the grey cobbled wynd
Tom caught my eye. Little Tommy Morrow,
whose father died in the Korean war.
He's apart from the fray, observing all,
a broken gun in one hand hanging down –
baggy shorts; stick-thin legs; a runny nose,

wearing wellies in summer.

George Watt

the music has seen to it[119]

I
concert hall: rapture in *Gaspard de la Nuit*
interrupted by a red-faced youth
who crashes through a stage side door
heard by all except Ravel's spirit ardent at his keys

II
she's still in bed: the window cleaner wakes her
dives under the covers to escape his rubbery smile
and his red-roped radio "Only the lonely
dum-dum-dum-dummy-do-wa"

III
two young lovers under a grand oak unaware of damp earth
make music of their own till an officer coughs
into the hand of the law a bare backside
loses tension and quivers no more

IV
mrs somerset stirs strawberry jam: sings
"upon the seat of a bicycle built…" but before "for two"
the angel of death takes shape in the steam above her head
she smiles drops to the hard slate floor with an a-musical
thump

V
somewhere
can be anywhere
maybe
confusion at a stage door
squeaks from a window squeegee
coitus interruptus
ghostly shapes in steam
a happy corpse on a floor

even when they are gone
finished in a way
they are always there
in that place
always
filling that ambient space
with so much more
than memory:
the music has seen to it.

George Watt

Treacle Toffee & the Grammar of Self[120]
From the Glasgow Poems:1959

A line of damp winter coats steam on hooks.
Radiators burp with dyspepsia.
Moisture runs on painted walls thick with time.
Schoolroom. Mrs Crawford. Brillo-pad bun,
pendulous breasts hang over a hard tray
of treacle toffee. Silver hammer poised.
Crack! Crack again! Each tasty, jagged piece
to the favoured few who know their grammar,
who take a line apart, award each word
its proper class in perfect cursive script

on a creamy page: light up, heavy down.
"You are a noun, pronoun, can be subject
or object! Pay attention!" But I can't.
Seductive is the small propeller plane
seen through the one high, clear pane of glass
amongst older, frosted others. It draws
a clean line across the rare winter blue,
its drone a purr and hum – now heard, then not,
and back. It takes so long to pass from sight,
its poignant diminuendo leaving

within a strange and abiding comfort.
The plane took me from my nominal bench
from my dull, imprisoned purported self
and I wandered at will: up, above, abroad. Away.
Decades on in my silver years, eyes closed,
the plane's consolatory purr is there now,
still calling me from the leaden mundane.
So I'm here, but there; I'm now and then,
more an adverb of place or time than noun.
With such a singular grammar, can there be
any hope for toffee for me?

George Watt

Winter Camp[121]

refugees queue stranded at this border crossing
perched in tents and other shambles
stuck between one country and another
where we are coming from and passing to

we drive in airconditioned comfort
all that slows our bus is traffic bunched and stalled
otherwise we cross unimpeded into the mountains
and our snowbound postcard village

there must be some reason they wait here
there's nothing stopping them
not the location or outlook
nor hunger in this abundant Europe

exhaustion perhaps simply running out
of what drove them or fear of what is in front of them
stranded between past and future
under the no vacancy sign

Michael Witts

To the Knees[122]

Who has the strongest knees?
Oh, he sure does

It's three a.m.
I rise in the darkness,
Just as he did after tossing and turning
Before walking through the town
To put a cross on the door
Of whoever deserved death

How could he be so merciless?
But this is what the holy book says.
Maybe he repented, as I will
For wanting to be so close to you
As he did to the obelisk of his belief

Towards the lilies of your pond
I pray to have the knees to move

Be careful of a man who's roaming
Like this one in a book I read:
He comes to the artist's ranch
To look for odd jobs
In return for water and food
But winds up being her slave
Like that other one in a show I watched:
A homeless man rescued by a priest –
He doesn't expect to be killed
In the same room where they make love

The mysterious knees keep them moving

Proud animals, all of them:
Either as an old angel with enormous wings
Who dropped accidentally onto a mucky country road,
His knees bent, badly wounded
Or as a dead young man
Whose body floated on the sea for years
Forever beautiful, not ever to rot
His knees stretching out, peace in the blue

You must've heard stories
Where kids kneel down before their parents
But who knows what happens
When parents kneel down before their children?
Even wild imagination fails this world
You see a crying mob get down on their knees
In front of the ruler for their life
But what if the other way around?
Before the execution
They cut the ligaments in his knees
So with gravity the despot will kneel down
In front of the maddening crowd

I'm talking about dignity and fate.
As they say, under your knees there is gold
You don't give it away for no good reason
Nor should you waste it to disgrace yourself

But now I am all on my knees, begging
Touch me, love

Zuo Fei
15 August 2020

THE POETS

The following brief biographies are based on texts provided by the poets. As there is an interval of months between the submission of brief biographies and the editing of the Anthology, much may have changed in the meantime.

VINITA AGRAWAL is the author of four books of poetry – *Two Full Moons* (Bombaykala Books), *Words Not Spoken* (Brown Critique), *The Longest Pleasure* (Finishing Line Press) and *The Silk Of Hunger* (AuthorsPress) – Vinita is a Mumbai based, award-winning poet and writer. She was Senior Editor with Womaninc.com for three years. Recipient of the Rabindranath Tagore Literary Prize 2018, Gayatri GaMarsh Memorial Award for Literary Excellence, USA, 2015, her poems have appeared in *Asiancha, Constellations, The Fox Chase Review, Pea River Journal, Lumen, Cyclamen And Swords, Open Road Review, Stockholm Literary Review, Poetry Pacific, Mithila Review, Chandrabhaga, Blue Fifth Review, The Bombay Review* and other journals and in anthologies from Australia, Ireland and Israel. She was nominated for the Best of the Net Awards in 2011. Her poem won a prize for the Moon Anthology on the Moon by TallGrass Writers Guild 2017. She was awarded first prize in the Wordweavers Contest 2014, commendation prize in the All India Poetry Competition 2014. She contributed a monthly column on Asian Poets on the literary blog of the Hamline university, Saint Paul, USA in 2016-17. She judged the RLFPA poetry contest (International Prize) in 2016 and co-judged *Asian Cha*'s poetry contest on The Other Side, in 2015. She has read at the FILEY Book Fair, Merida, Mexico, Kala Ghoda Arts Festival, Lucknow Literary festival, Cappuccino Readings and Women Empowerment events. She is on the Advisory Board of the Tagore Literary Prize. She co-curates events for PEN Mumbai and sub-curates for the Kala Ghoda Literary Festival.

JOY C. AL-SOFI is a published writer of poetry, fiction and non-fiction. Originally from the USA, where she was a practicing attorney, she has been teaching English in Hong Kong since 2004.

SHIKHA BANSAL has worked in the publishing industry for several years both in India and Hong Kong. She currently resides in India.

ANDREW BARKER spent his youth working as bricklayer before entering academia and obtaining an Honors Degree in English Literature, an MA in Anglo/Irish Literature and a PhD in American Literature. He now works as a university literature lecturer in Hong Kong and releases poetry online through his poetry web channel mycroftlectures.com. His online Mycroft Lectures on poetry are popular with a wide range of netizens, and he is the author of *Snowblind from my Protective Colouring* (2010), and *Joyce is Not Here: 101 Modern Shakespearean Sonnets*, (2017) and the forthcoming *Orange Peel: Modern Shakespearean Sonnets 102-203*.

GARY BEAUMIER, in his later years, has become something of a beachcomber and has self diagnosed with "compulsive walking disorder." On a number of occasions he has cobbled together wooden sailboats. He is a finalist and semi finalist for the Luminaire Award for several of his poems and a finalist for the Joy Bale Boone award and was nominated for Best of the Net Award for his poem Rio Grande. He won *Streetlight Magazine*'s 1st Prize for his poem 'Night Train to Paris'. He won first prize for his poem 'Night Forest' with *Flying Ketchup Press*. His work has appeared in numerous other publications. His chapbook *From My Family to Yours* has been published by Finishing Line Press. His second book of poetry *Dented Brown Fedora* has been published by Uncollected Press. He once taught poetry in a women's prison.

ALAN BERN is a retired Children's Librarian from the Berkeley Public Library. He worked in public libraries in the San Francisco Bay Area for over 25 years in a variety of jobs. He is a poet, storywriter, and photographer and has two books of poetry published by Fithian Press: *No no the saddest* (2004) and *Waterwalking in Berkeley* (2007). A third book of poetry, *greater distance and other poems* (2015), was published by his own press, Lines & Faces, a press and publisher specializing in illustrated poetry broadsides, collaborating with the artist Robert Woods, linesandfaces.com. Alan was a runner up for

The Raw Art Review's The John H. Kim Memorial Short Fiction Prize for his story 'The alleyway near the downtown library'; and he won a medal from SouthWest Writers for his story 'The Return of the Very Fierce Wolf of Gubbio to Assisi, 1943 CE [and now, 2013 CE]' and his poem 'Boxae' was first runner-up for the Raw Art Review's first Mirabai Prize for Poetry, 2020. He was also a finalist in the NCWN's 2019 Thomas Wolfe Fiction Prize; he won the Littoral Press Poetry Prize in 2015; and he was a semi-finalist in the 2016 Center for the Book Arts Poetry Chapbook Competition. Alan has poems, stories, and photos published in a wide variety of online and print publications, from which his work has been nominated for Pushcart Prizes.

Recent photos published include: unearthedesf.com/alan-bern, feralpoetry.net/four-haiga-by-alan-bern/, and pleaseseeme.com/issue-7/art/alan-bern-art-psm7/.

Alan is also a performer working with the dancer Lucinda Weaver as PACES: dance & poetry fit to the space and with musicians from Composing Together, http://composingtogether.org/index.php/programs/ http://composingtogether.org/index.php/sample-poetry-from-our-musical-storytime-performances/ http://composingtogether.org/index.php/programs/ http://composingtogether.org/index.php/sample-poetry-from-our-musical-storytime-performances/

THEA BIESHEUVEL is currently a resident of Australia, although born in the Netherlands. It took a while for her to master the English language but she now has four publications to her name. Her passion is poetry but short stories come a close second. She can be found in a Google search or in Smashwords and other on-line publications.

LIAM BLACKFORD is a West Australian poet living and working in Hong Kong. He is of millennial age. He was born and grew up in suburban Perth. He has previously lived in Perth and Shanghai. He writes poetry in English and Chinese. He holds a degree in law and philosophy. His poems are written in a fixed form and meter and are concerned with themes of truth and reality, complexity and change, anxiety and rage, and power and control.

MARIA ELENA BLANCO, poet, essayist and translator born in Havana (Cuba) writes predominantly in her native Spanish. Having spent a good part of her formative years in New York, she translates her own poetry into English and has developed her own distinct English poetic voice. Published poetry: *Posesión por pérdida* (1990), *Corazón sobre la tierra / tierra en los Ojos* (1998), *Alquímica memoria* (2001), *Mitologuías* (2001), *danubiomediterráneo /mittelmeerdonau* (2005), *El amor incontable (*2008), *Havanity / Habanidad* (English-Spanish anthology, 2010), *Sobresalto al vacío* (2015) and the anthologies *Escrito en lenguas* (2015, 2017), *Botín* (2016), *De parte de nadie* (2016) and *Oro vano* (2018). In German translation: *Wilde Lohe* (2007) and *Sprung ins Blaue* (2016, bilingual German-Spanish). Essays: *Asedios al texto literario* (1999, literary criticism) and *Devoraciones. Ensayos de período especial* (2016, Cuban culture and politics). Poetry translations from French (Charles Baudelaire) and German (G. Kofler and M.-T. Kerschbaumer, among others). Winner of First (2019), Second (2016) and Third (2017, 2018) prizes in the International Proverse Poetry Prize (Single Poems), Hong Kong, as well as other international poetry distinctions. Lives mainly in Vienna (Austria).

GAVIN BOURKE has worked in public service for over twenty years. He grew up in the suburb of Tallaght, in West Dublin and lives in County Meath. He holds a B.A. in Humanities from Dublin City University, an M.A. in Modern Drama Studies and a Higher Diploma in Information Studies, from University College Dublin. His work broadly covers nature, time, memory, addiction, mental health, human relationships, the inner and outer life, creating meaning and purpose, politics, contemporary and historical social issues, injustice, the human situation, power and its abuse, as well as urban and rural life, personal autonomy, ethics, in English and to a lesser extent, in the Irish Language. He has participated in many national and international poetry competitions, with both single poems and book-length collections winning some and being shortlisted and/or highly commended in others. He has been published internationally in various literary journals and has participated in literary festivals. Gavin is also a multi-instrumentalist and has been a songwriter and composer for the past thirty years.

LAWRENCE BRIDGES best known in America for work in the film and literary world. His poetry has appeared in *The New Yorker*, *Poetry*, *The Tampa Review*, and *Ambit*. He has published three volumes of poetry, *Horses on Drums*, *Flip Days*, and *Brownwood*. He created a series of literary documentaries for the National Endowment for the Arts 'Big Read' initiative, which includes profiles of Ray Bradbury, Amy Tan, Tobias Wolff and Cynthia Ozick. He lives in Los Angeles.

LINA BUIVIDAVICIUTE was born on May 14, 1986. She has a BA in Lithuanian philology and advertising, and a MA in Lithuanian literature. She is a poet, literary scholar and literary critic. Her first poetry book *Helsinki Syndrome* was published in 2017.

VINCENT CASAREGOLA teaches American literature and film, creative writing, rhetorical studies, and composition. He has published poetry in a number of journals, including *The Bellevue Review*, *The Examined Life*, *Natural Bridge*, WLA, *Dappled Things*, *2River*, *Work*, *Lifelines*, and *Blood and Thunder*. He has also published creative nonfiction and flash fiction.

TOM K.E. CHAN holds an MFA in Creative Writing at the University of Hong Kong, where he also holds his BA in Language and Communication. He is an active poet for PoetryOutLoud Hong Kong and Peel Street Poetry. His poems have published in the Proverse Poetry Prize (single poems) 2020 Anthology, *Mingled Voices 5*, 聲韻詩刊 *Voice & Verse Poetry Magazine* and *Cha: An Asian Literary Journal*. Currently, Tom is writing a series of short stories and a poetry collection set in the carnivalesque city of Hong Kong.

MARGARET CLARKE spent her early professional life teaching English in a grammar school in Liverpool. After marrying she moved with her husband to Newcastle Upon

Tyne and then to Glasgow. When all her children were at school, she returned to teaching, moving later into a post at Notre Dame College of Education in Glasgow. The college eventually became part of the University of Glasgow.

When her husband, whose special interest was in Futuristic Fiction, was asked to prepare a new edition of a work entitled *The Last Man*, his researches revealed that what purported to be an English text was in fact an unacknowledged translation of a French work by Jean-Baptiste François Xavier Cousin De Grainville, published in 1806. That fact, of course, was of interest. The quality of the translation left much to be desired and the Wesleyan University Press asked Margaret to provide a new one which her husband would edit. Success there led to a request for a translation of *Le Monde Tel Qu'il Sera,* a look into the future by Émile Souvestre, published in 1846. Since her husband was busy, Margaret translated this book with the title *The World As It Shall Be.*

In retirement Margaret has enjoyed working with Gillian and Verner Bickley and providing Prefaces for the *Mingled Voices* series of anthologies.

WILLIAM LEO COAKLEY's poems have been published for many years in magazines, anthologies, and newspapers at home and abroad (including China, England, and Ireland). He often gives public readings, especially at the Poetry Society in London and the Leslie-Lohman Museum of Art and the Irish American Writers and Artists theatre in New York and on the radio in Montreal and Boston.

His poems have won awards in the Arvon Foundation Sotheby's International Poetry Competition in England, the Yeats Society in New York, and the New England Poetry Club.

For the last two years in Ireland (where he is also a citizen) he has been on the shortlist for the New Irish Writing Prize, with the selected poems being published in the *Irish Times.*

AUDREY COLASANTI has been shortlisted for the Anne Sexton Prize For Poetry and the Sandy Crimmons National Prize. She was also a semi-finalist for the 2020 Walt Whitman Award/*Graywolf Press* and long-listed for the Poetry Society 2020 National Poetry Competition. Her poems have been featured in *The Earth Journal, Wingless Dreamer, Button Eye Review, Inkwell Literary Magazine, Tiny Seed Literary Journal, MPR Minnesota Public Radio, Humana Obscura*, amongst others.

SUZANNE COTTRELL, an Ohio buckeye by birth, lives with her husband in rural Piedmont, North Carolina. An outdoor enthusiast and retired teacher, she enjoys reading, writing, hiking, knitting, Pilates, Tai Chi, and yoga. Her poems have appeared in numerous journals and anthologies including *Avocet, Poetry Quarterly, The Pangolin Review, Burningword Literary Journal* and *Mingled Voices*. She's the author of two poetry chapbooks: *Gifts of the Seasons, Autumn and Winter* and *Gifts of the Seasons, Spring and Summer*, published by Kelsay Books. She was the recipient of the 2017 Rebecca Lard Poetry Award, Prolific Press.

ALECIA C. DANTICO is a digital strategist by day, a communications professor by night, and an emerging creative writer in the crevices, trying to rework the order of those clauses. Her micro-bio says it best: writer, introvert, bookworm, feminist, scholar, francophile, oenophile, professor, activist, geek.

LAWDENMARC DECAMORA is a Best of the Net and Pushcart Prize-nominated Filipino writer with work published in 23 countries around the world. He is the author of two book-length poetry collections, 'TUNNELS' (India: Ukiyoto Publishing) and *Love, Air* (USA: Atmosphere Press). His work has appeared in *Seattle Review, North Dakota Quarterly, The Common, The Margins*, among other places. He was long-listed for The Alpine Fellowship Writing Prize 2021 (UK), appeared on the shortlist of "Asia Pacific of the Mind," an Asia Pacific Writers & Translators/Joao Roque Literary Journal publication collaboration, as well as earning an honourable mention on the special Love 2018 issue of *Columbia Journal* (Columbia U, New York). He also won a spot in various anthologies, most recently in *Meridian: The APWT Drunken Boat Anthology of New Writing* and *Mingled Voices 4: The International Proverse Poetry Prize Anthology 2019*. He was selected to participate at the Tupelo 30/30 Project of Tupelo Press as an August 2021 volunteer poet.

NEIL DOUGLAS is a doctor who has worked as a GP and a Community Paediatrician in London's East End. He is an enthusiastic member of the Covent Garden Stanza poetry collective affiliated with the Poetry Society and has published work in the UK, North America and Hong Kong. In 2020 he was longlisted for the Poetry Society's National Poetry Competition and in 2021 was shortlisted for the Bridport Prize. He is currently studying for an MA in Creative and Life Writing at Goldsmiths, University of London.

ALLY ELLIOTT is a primary school teacher in the United Kingdom, who writes poetry in her spare time at home.

D. W. EVANS was born in Newcastle upon Tyne. First study, then work took him south to London, then Brighton and eventually Jersey. 'Discharged Wednesday' won the Alan Jones Memorial Prize 2019. 'Rapunzel' was selected for a prize and appeared in *A3 Review* (April 2020 edition). 'La Rue des Touettes' was shortlisted for the 7th Ó Bhéal Five Words Poetry Competition, and published in *Five Words*, Vol. XIII. 'Turnips' was, highly commended in the first Acumen International Poetry Competition 2019/20.

ADELE EVERSHED is originally from Wales. She has lived in both Hong Kong and Singapore before settling in Connecticut USA. Adele has only recently turned her hand to writing poetry. She likes to write verse influenced by her experience of living in different countries and has poetry published by Didcot Writers and the journal, *Three Drops From A Cauldron*. Adele has had her flash fiction stories published by a variety of online journals. She recently was a semi-finalist in the London Independent Story Project competition and has had a story featured in the anthology, *Museum*, published by Enliven Press.

RYAN FENTON grew up in the United States, and he now lives in Hong Kong.

DANIELA FISCHEROVÁ was born in 1948 in Prague. She is a playwright, novelist, screenwriter, poet, children's author (IBBY – International Board on Books for Young People – 2016 Honours List). Wife, mother, grandmother.

CASEY HAMPTON is a poet and fiction writer currently residing in the Pacific Northwest. His work has appeared in *Dialogue*, *Entropy*, *Star 82 Review*, *Euphony Journal* and elsewhere. When not writing, he helps out on the family farm and spends as much time as he can with his coonhound Josie.

CARRIE HOOPER was born and raised in Elmira, New York. She received a Bachelor's degree in music performance from Mansfield University and Master's degrees in German and vocal performance from the State University of New York at Buffalo. She studied one year at the Royal University College of Music in Stockholm, Sweden as a Fulbright Scholar. Carrie taught German, Italian, and Romanian between 2002 and 2019 at Elmira College (Elmira, New York). She teaches voice and piano lessons, sings in a local chorus, gives vocal concerts, and plays the piano and organ at a church. She has published two collections of poetry and has translated a book, articles, and short stories from Albanian and Romanian into English.

R. J. KEELER was born in St. Paul, Minnesota, and grew up in the jungles of Colombia. He holds a BS in Mathematics from North Carolina State University, an MS in Computer Science from the University of North Carolina-Chapel Hill, an MBA from the University of California at Los Angeles, and a Certificate in Poetry from the University of Washington. An Honorman in the U.S. Naval Submarine School, he was Submarine Service (SS) qualified. He is a recipient of the Vietnam Service Medal, Honorable Discharge, and a Whiting Foundation Experimental Grant. He is a member of IEEE (technological society), AAAS (scientific society), and the Academy of American Poets. A former Boeing engineer.

His first poetry collection, *Detonation*, has recently been published by Wipf and Stock.

CHRISTOS KOUKIS was born in 1979 and he is a poet and a writer. He has published poetry books in Greece, France, India and Serbia and poems of his have been translated in several languages. He has participated in poetry anthologies in Greece and other countries and in international poetry festivals around the world. He has worked in poetry and culture magazines and has written lyrics for songs. Also he collaborated in an international project for Documenta 14 Athens. He is the director of an international poetry festival in Greece. He lives and works in Athens.

LYNDA MCKINNEY LAMBERT lives in western Pennsylvania, USA. She is a retired professor of fine art and humanities, Geneva College, Beaver Falls, PA. Since retirement from her teaching schedule, she can devote her time every day to writing poetry and non-fiction essays. She has four published books available on Amazon at this time. Her themes are nature, seasons, passage of time, Pilgrimage, and she is inspired by literature, music, and dance. Lynda writes spare poems and thoughtful personal essays. She writes, "I love nature, the heavenlies, walking my dogs, taking care of feral cats, standing in a meadow on a windy day with wildflowers all around me, and watching the sky in the middle of the night in winter.
Poetry is life. I fell in love with poetry as an undergraduate fine arts major. From the beginning, I was hooked. It's a wonder-filled life."

SUSAN LAVENDER is published poet, actress, radio newsreader, voice acting coach, yoga practitioner and retired solicitor. She performs in theatre, film, story-telling and literary events, such as the Hong Kong Literary Festival, and for fund-raising events for causes such as diversity and LGBTQI rights, often writing her own material and incorporating yoga into her performances.
Anglo-Italian by birth, Sue has lived in Hong Kong and China for 29 years. She has also lived in the U.K., Canada, Italy and Romania. She is bilingual in English and Italian, fluent in French and has studied Mandarin in Beijing and Cantonese in Hong Kong. In addition to two law degrees (LL.B. and B.C.L. from McGill University, Montreal), Sue has a 1st Class Hons. degree from University College London in Italian and Romanian.

J. P. LINSTROTH lives in the United States and has been writing poetry since he was a boy. He obtained a D.Phil. in Social and Cultural Anthropology from the University of Oxford and is an Adjunct Professor at Barry University and Faculty Member at the Catholic University of New Spain (UCNE). His books include: *Marching Against Gender Practice: Political Imaginings in the Basqueland* (2015, Lexington Books), *The Forgotten Shore* (Poetic Matrix Press, 2017), and *Epochal Reckonings* (Proverse Hong Kong, 2020, Winner of the 2019 Proverse Prize). Linstroth was a signatory of the Brussels Declaration for Peace to end ETA violence (2010). He was a co-recipient of an Alexander von Humboldt Foundation Grant (2005-2007) to study immigrant populations: Cubans, Haitians, and Guatemalan-Mayan immigrants in South Florida. He was awarded a J. William Fulbright Foreign Scholar Grant (2008-2009) to study urban Amerindians in Manaus, Brazil and to be a Visiting Professor at the Universida de Federal do Amazonas (UFAM). In 2017, he was awarded a Presidential Lifetime Achievement Award. Linstroth is a member of the Board of Directors of the International Peace Research Association Foundation (IPRAF). In 2019, he received a medal as a Gentleman of Merit and was inducted into La Noble Compañia de Bernardo de Gálvez (The Noble Order of Bernardo de Galvez). In addition to many academic articles, he writes opinion editorials (Op-Eds) in many newspapers and online news sources, including *CounterPunch*, *Des Moine Register*, *Euroscientist*, *L.A. Progressive*, *PeaceVoice*, *The Houston Chronicle*, and *Londonderry Sentinel*. His academic research interests are cognition, ethno-nationalism, gender, genocide, history, immigrant advocacy, indigeneity, indigenous politics, indigenous rights, love, memory, minority rights, peace, peace-building, racism, social justice, and trauma.

IRIS LITT's newest book of poems is *Snowbird* from Finishing Line Press. Previous books are *What I Wanted to Say* from Shivastan Press, and *Word Love* from Cosmic Trend Publications. A recent short story publication is, 'Pissed Off', in the *Saturday Evening Post* Fiction Contest Anthology. She has had short stories, poems and articles in *Saturday Evening Post, Travelers' Tales, Confrontation, The Widow's Handbook,*

The London Magazine, the new renaissance, Earth's Daughters, Rambunctious Review and many others. Awards include the *Atlantic Monthly* Award for College Writing, first prize in The Virtual Press short story contest, French Bread poetry award from *Pacific Coast Journal*. She was a finalist in the Valiant Literature 2020 Chapbook Contest. She has taught creative writing as an adjunct at SUNY/Ulster, Bard College, Arts Society of Kingston, Writers in the Mountains, New York Public Library and many other venues in New York City and the Hudson Valley. She lives in Woodstock, NY and winters on Anna Maria Island in Florida, which was the inspiration for 'Snowbird'.

S. E. LUDAN As an American Foreign Service Officer, S. E. Ludan has lived and worked in many different countries. S. E. Ludan began writing poetry several years ago.

K. B. RYAN JOSHUA MAHINDAPALA was born in 1991 in Singapore and graduated from the University of Liverpool with a bachelor's degree in Law in 2016. He was admitted to the Singapore Bar in 2020. He is a published writer of fiction, non-fiction and poetry. His work is an expression of his thoughts, feelings and opinions on current affairs, globalisation and history. He is an entrepreneur and the Founder/ Editor of *Thinking Movement*, a Medium publication centred around the formulation of strategic solutions in the areas of sustainability, social justice, inclusion, mental health and self-help with an Asian perspective. Ryan is an advocate for the promotion of arts, culture and sport. He is actively involved in numerous not-for-profit organisations where he provides his expertise in the area of social outreach, governance, law and strategy formulation. He is a management committee member of the Peranakan Indian Association of Singapore and a member of the Technical Committee of the Triathlon Association of Singapore where he is their social media lead strategist. Currently, Ryan is pursuing his postgraduate studies in Business Administration at the University of Strathclyde, United Kingdom. His work has been published on the Strathclyde Business School Blog, StrathUnion and the Strathclyde Telegraph. He draws inspiration from the people around him, his environment, past experiences, political figures and extensive travels around the world.

WAYNE PAUL MATTINGLY is a multi-award-winning playwright whose work has been staged in NYC; Westchester & Putnam Counties, N.Y; Los Angeles, San Francisco; Bangor, Maine; Denton & Houston, Texas; Chamblee, GA; Valdez, Alaska; Kauai, Hawaii; and London, England.

Winner of the Tennessee Chapbook Prize; Arts & Letters Prize in Drama, Finalist, Milledgeville, GA; Denton Community Theatre, Method and Madness Competition & Festival, Third Prize, Denton, TX; The Last Frontier Theatre Conference,/Susan Nims Distinguished Play Playwright Award Finalist, Valdez, Alaska; Phoenix Theatre, Hormel New Play Festival Finalist; The Ashland New Plays Festival Semi-finalist, Ashland, OR; Ronald Duncan Literary Prize Finalist, United Kingdom; 25th Annual International Playwriting Festival, Snapshot Production, Warehouse Theatre Co., London, U.K. and an IATC Cimientos Play Development Program Finalist, NYC.

He is a proud recipient of the 2020 BRIO Award; 2014 Helene Wurlitzer Foundation Fellowship Artists Residency Grant, Taos, NM; & to be a Grant Recipient of the 2014 & 2015 Disquiet International Literary Programs (short plays) in Lisbon, Portugal; and a 2015/16 & 2017/18 Can Serrat International Artists Residency Grant Recipient, in Barcelona, Spain.

He was a founding member & Dramaturg of The Misfits Ensemble, L.A.: Founding Artistic Director, Tiger's Heart Players, N.Y: a Dramatist Guild, & AEA member. Last stage appearance: 2013 Midtown International Theatre Festival, NYC, nominated for a Best Lead Actor Award. He has also directed dozens of works in both CA & NY. His latest full-length drama, *Anthem*, received reads with The Village Playwrights, NYC & Axial Theatre, Ossining, NY.

His work has appeared in the following publications: 2020, *Mingled Voices 4*; *2020 Best 10-Minute Plays*; *2014 Best Women's Monologues*; *1999 Best Women's Monologues & Best Stage Scenes*, Smith & Kraus. *More 10-Minute Plays for Teens*, 2015, Applause Theatre & Cinema Books: and 2007

Poetry & Plays 14. Limited work is available at National New Play Network: nnpn.org.

JACK MAYER is a Vermont writer and pediatrician. His was the first pediatric practice in Eastern Franklin County, on the Canadian border, where he began writing essays, poems and short stories about his practice and hiking Vermont's Long Trail. He was a country doctor for ten years, often bartering medical care for eggs, firewood, and knitted afghans. From 1987 to 1991 Dr Mayer was a National Cancer Institute Fellow at Columbia University researching the molecular biology of cancer. Dr Mayer established Rainbow Pediatrics in Middlebury, Vermont in 1991 where he continues to practice primary care pediatrics. He is an Instructor in Pediatrics at the University of Vermont School of Medicine and an adjunct faculty for pre-medical students at Middlebury College. He was a participant at the Bread Loaf Writers' Conference in 2003 and 2005 (fiction) and 2008 (poetry). His first non-fiction book is *Life In A Jar: The Irena Sendler Project*. His new book, *Before The Court Of Heaven*, is historical fiction about the rise of Nazism, and has received 14 book awards. His collection of poems inspired and composed in wilderness, *Poems From The Wilderness*, was published in Nov. 2020 and won the International Proverse Prize 2019.

RIANKA MOHAN is a writer living in Beijing. Her work has been featured on the Spittoon podcast and their megacity event in 2019 as well as The Glasshouse Literary Festival, India in 2020. She has moderated panels at the Beijing Bookworm Literary Festival, the EU-China Literature Festival, and CultureConnect, among others. Before China, she spent three years in Bangkok where she was the Arts and Culture Editor for *The Expat Life* magazine and wrote a monthly music column for *Bangkok 101*. Prior to that, she spent 15 years in New York working as an investment banker for JPMorgan and Credit Suisse.

GLÓRIA SOFIA MONTEIRO "is a dreamer as most poets. Born in the city of Praia in Cape Verde, Gloria shares her dreams with her two children. She graduated in Engineering and Environmental Management in the Azores, another place that she cherishes for allowing her to continue to be an islander. Ever fascinated by writing, she has played with words since she was a child, exchanging dolls for diaries, and finding comfort when her secrets and thoughts are guarded in a white page.

Gloria's poems capture moments of her journey and are full of passion and the emotions as the author herself. Gloria has grown to make her voice heard in different arenas, believing that in addition to writing about feelings she also needs to speak, shout or take action on some realities. Among other poetry sites she collaborates with the online newspaper of magazines in the world. She was nominated to apply for RMAPAI. She has been invited by 3 University from Boston (April 2019). Harvard University, Tufts University and Boston University for reading and conversation about genre and literature. She's also represented her country Cape Verde in VIII Conference in Portuguese Language Literature UMass Boston, gala ciudad la paz Bolivia 2020.

Her poetry has been translated into more than 15 languages, in 2020 she won a prize for Union Mundial Poetas Paz Liberdade She participated in International Poetry Festivals in Curtea de Arges, Romania (2016), Istanbul, Turkey (2017), Ditet & Naimit, Macedonia / Albania (2018), and the festival internacional Bangladesh.

Her published books are:

Lacos de Poesias, Editora Brial, Rotterdam, Holanda, 2015
Abriel, Editora Brial, Rotterdam, Holanda, 2018
Urso Haby, United P.C, Rotterdam, Holanda, 2019
Mar de Cabo Verde, Vakxikon Publications, Atenas, Greece, 2021."

NATALIE NERA is a pen name of Natalie Dunn. She is a Czech writer, an author of two published novels as well as an editor of a poetry anthology in her mother tongue, who spent fifteen years in the UK with her British husband and children but has recently relocated to Prague. She writes in Czech, English and occasionally translates. Her written work has appeared in Czech, Russian, German, English, Bengali, Spanish and Romanian. Her work has appeared, for example, in *Mslexia, Eunoia Review, The Selkie, Litero Mania* and *Tvar*. She is Prose Editor and Co-Founder of *Fragmented Voices*, a small independent press based in Newcastle-upon-Tyne, United Kingdom, and Prague, Czech Republic. In January 2021, Natalie became a member of the Czech Centre of the International Pen Club.

PHILIP NOURSE was born in Wells, Somerset. He was educated at St George's School, Windsor Castle, and Marlborough College before reading psychology at Brunel University. After qualifying as a chartered surveyor, he worked in London and Hong Kong where he and his second wife, Diane, lived for thirty-three years. In 2005, Philip began a new career in publishing and also set up his own business, offering editorial, design and photography services. He and Diane returned to live in London in 2017, although they keep a pied-à-terre in Hong Kong to escape the English winters.

DENISE O'HAGAN was born in Rome and based in Sydney. She has a background in commercial book publishing, and worked as an editor for Collins, Heinemann, Routledge and Cambridge University Press, and was consulting editor for the State Library of NSW. In 2015 she set up her own imprint, Black Quill Press, through which she assists authors wishing to publish independently. She is also Poetry Editor for Australia/New Zealand for the Irish literary journal *The Blue Nib*. Her poetry is widely published and awarded. Her awards include the Dalkey Poetry Prize (2020), first prize in the Adelaide Plains Poetry Competition (2019), second prize in the Sutherland Shire Literary Competition, shortlisting in the Saolta Arts Poetry Competition, the Booranga Literary Prizes and the Robert Graves Poetry Prize. *The Beating Heart* is her debut poetry collection (Ginninderra Press 2020).

HELEN OLIVER is an ESL teacher, materials writer and editor. She taught at the British Council in Hong Kong from 1978 - 1980, then lived and taught in Japan for 15 years, before returning to work in New Zealand. Working part-time now means she has more time for tai chi, music, books and poetry, family and friends. She loves the sea, kayaking and wandering the beaches of the Coromandel. Writing is becoming a passion. Having a poem published in *Mingled Voices 4*: *International*

Proverse Poetry Prize Anthology 2019 was her first international achievement.

RENA ONG is an English lady, married with one son, and lives in Singapore. There are many parks that she loves to wander around and she is delighted that her home is near the Singapore Botanical and Heritage Gardens, where one finds works of art and snippets of history amongst the beautiful landscapes, the historical and contemporary meeting in harmony.

JUN (JANICE) PAN is an interpreter, researcher, and interpreter trainer. With a passion for reading and writing, she founded a Chinese poetry club and published a couple of Chinese poems (shi and ci) at the age of twelve at her birthplace in Xiangtan, Hunan. She then studied English language and literature in Jiangsu, and then, interpreting in Shanghai. She came to Hong Kong in 2008 for her PhD in interpreting studies and has been teaching interpreting and translation at local tertiary institutions since then.

Jun has worked as an interpreter (and translator) for many years, although her childhood dream was to become a writer, film director or painter. She found her childhood immersion in Chinese classic literature and culture important and invaluable in her life and career. Apart from introducing Chinese culture to many of her clients when she worked as an interpreter, Jun also participated in the translation of several classic works from English to Chinese, including John Ruskin's five-volume *Modern Painters*, Lyman Frank Baum's *The Wonderful Wizard of Oz* and *The Marvelous Land of Oz*, etc.

Jun is now Associate Professor in the Department of Translation, Interpreting and Intercultural Studies at Hong Kong Baptist University, and was recently a visiting Faculty member at the State University of New York at Binghamton.

Although PETER PARLE left school with no formal qualifications, he enjoyed a 42-year career working on Military Aircraft. Firstly he had a 25-year career with the Royal Air Force as a Safety & Survival Equipment specialist, including

Aircrew Clothing. Secondly he was employed by a civilian Aerospace company as a Quality and Airworthiness Specialist.

He is married and has been for 45 years, he has one son. He enjoys puzzles, quizzes and reading crime fiction. He holds a season ticket for Liverpool Football Club's home Premiership games.

JOANNA RADWANSKA-WILLIAMS was born in Warsaw, Poland, and spent a part of her childhood in London, England. She received her B.A. with a double major in English and Linguistics (awarded with Highest Honors) and her Ph.D. in Linguistics from the University of North Carolina at Chapel Hill. Her dissertation was published as *A Paradigm Lost: The Linguistic Theory of Miko'aj Kruszewski* (Amsterdam: John Benjamins, 1993). She taught Slavic Linguistics (Polish and Russian) at the State University of New York at Stony Brook (1989-1994) and the University of Illinois at Chicago (1994-1995), and English Linguistics at Nanjing University (1996-1999) and the Chinese University of Hong Kong (1999-2003). In 2003, she joined Macao Polytechnic Institute, where she is now a full professor at the MPI-Bell Centre of English.

Joanna's poetry has been anthologized in several collections, including *Lingua Franca: An Anthology of Poetry by Linguists* (edited by Donna Jo Napoli and Emily Norwood Rando; Lake Bluff, Illinois: Jupiter Press, 1989), *Montage of Life* (Owings Mills, Maryland: The National Library of Poetry, 1998), *I Roll the Dice: Contemporary Macao Poetry* (edited by Christopher Kit Kelen and Agnes Vong; Macao: Association of Stories in Macao, 2008), *Lotus Field 2018: Reflections* (edited by Zi-yu Lin, Joanna Radwanska-Williams and Yunfeng Zhang; Macao: Macao Polytechnic Institute, 2018), *Mingled Voices 2: International Proverse Poetry Prize Anthology 2017*, *Mingled Voices 3: International Proverse Poetry Prize Anthology 2018*, *Mingled Voices 4: International Proverse Poetry Prize Anthology 2019* (edited by Gillian Bickley and Verner Bickley; Hong Kong: Proverse Hong Kong, 2018, 2019, 2020), and *Songs for Salamanders* (edited by Cat Dossett; Boston: Pen & Anvil Press, 2020).

C. N. RAJALAKSHMI (RAJI) is a poet and Language Teacher living in Hong Kong with her family. Her facebook page,

"Raji's Poetic World", attracts an international audience. Raji's poetry explores culture and nature with deep underlying philosophies, inspired by human nature, religion and natural sceneries. For her, "Poetry is an artistic expression of the self". Her poems have appeared in various international anthologies and online platforms and she has read her work on RTHK.

M. ANN REED is a researcher, poet, Chinese calligrapher-brush painter and professor of English Literature and Theory of Knowledge. She has taught in Malaysia, Ukraine, Bosnia-Herzegovina and China where traditional cultures regard literature a medical art. Her postdoctoral research studies the mending arts of English poetry and drama. Her Chinese calligraphy and brush paintings have been exhibited in Portland, Oregon and at the Shenzhen Fine Arts Museum in China. Her poems have been published in various literary journals. Her chapbook, *making oxygen, remaining inside this pure hollow note*, has been recently released by Finishing Line Press.

VINNI C. RELWANI lives in Singapore, calling it home for the last 20 years, with a soft-spot for Hong Kong where she was born and raised. A homemaker and mum, Vinni enjoys writing, and is in her zone when writing poetry and short stories.

JOSE MANUEL SEVILLA was born in Barcelona in 1959 and has been living in Hong Kong since 2003.
His published poetry books (in Spanish) are: *From the limits of paradise (1991), Alice in Ikea's Catalogue, The Night of Europe* (2004), *Ashes of Auschwitz and Eighteen Dogs* (awarded the Angel Urrutia award in 2009), and *Family Album (2016).*
His English-language poetry collection, *The Year of the Apparitions*, was published by Proverse Hong Kong in 2020.
His plays for the theatre are: "El Puente" / "The Bridge" (written after a trip to Croatia during the last European war, and staged in Catalonia, Spain (2000) and Hong Kong (2011), "Sombras, Sol y Flamenco" (Ballet by Ingrid Sera-Gilet, Hong Kong), 2012 and "Kennedy" 2016.

His poem, 'Sonia Wants to Rent an Apartment' won first prize in the Asian Cha Poetry Contest, "Encountering", in 2012 . His group of poems, "Of Words and Keys" was included in the Proverse Prize 2017 anthology *Mingled Voices 2*, his poem, 'Voice and Verse', in the *Asian Cha* Tenth Anniversary Anthology (2018) and his poem, 'The Talking Photo' in *Mingled Voices 3* (2019).

His work has also appeared in Spanish-language anthologies, *Trayecto contiguo* (1993) and *Otro Canto* (2013).

DALE SHANK's fiction and poetry have been published in: *Wingless Dreamer, Exquisite Corpse, The Healing Muse, The Raw Art Review, Akros Review, Before the Sun, Croton Review, Joint Endeavor, Powder*, and *University of Portland Review*.

ALLEGRA JOSTAD SILBERSTEIN grew up on a farm in Wisconsin but has lived in California since 1963. Her love of poetry began as a child when her mother would recite poems as she worked. Now that she is retired there is more time for singing and dancing as well as poetry. She has three chapbooks of poetry. In the spring of 2015, Cold River Press published her first book and she is widely published in journals such as *Blue Unicorn, California Quarterly, Iodine Poetry* and *Poetry Now*. In March of 2010 she was honored to become the first Poet Laureate for the city of Davis, CA.

HAYLEY ANN SOLOMON is an author, librarian and poet. She has been particularly fortunate during the course of her writing career and has thoroughly enjoyed her excursions into multiple genres – fiction fantasy, literary short stories, poetry, historical romance and even the odd non-fiction academic article. She is very grateful to Proverse Hong Kong, who has recognised her several times in the past, in particular the 2017 and 2018 Supplementary Prizes in the annual Proverse Prize. Poetry is one of Hayley's particular interests – she enjoys the vehicle for succinct delivery of philosophy, sonic beauty and metric rhythms.

Her Poetry collection, *Celestial Promise* (Proverse 2017) – available through Amazon and the Chinese University of Hong Kong Press, Hong Kong – encapsulates her view of the beauty of poetry as a medium for expression – the variability of mood, meter, rhythm, theme, philosophy, high jinx and emotional resonance in juxtaposition or synergy, perhaps, with the constraints of form.

Hayley is the mother of a lawyer, a scientist and a software engineer. She is the wife of a surgeon and is, in her spare time, a classical soprano. She is studying for her ATCL in music and sings with the Marlborough Singers, so her life is a rather eclectic potpourri of different thoughts, viewpoints and momentum!

ABBIE JOHNSON TAYLOR is the author of a romance novel, two poetry collections, and a memoir and hopes to publish another novel this year. Her work appears in *The Weekly Avocet*, *Magnets and Ladders*, and other publications. She is visually impaired and lives in Sheridan, Wyoming, where for six years, she cared for her late husband, who was totally blind and partially paralyzed by two strokes.

LUISA TERNAU was born and raised in Trieste, Northeastern Italy. After graduating at the University of Trieste she moved to the UK (London and one year in Wales). She obtained an MA in English Literature at King's College, University of London. Since then Luisa has lived in a number of countries across three continents. She has been based in Hong Kong for the last ten years. Luisa likes to write poems and short stories. Her inspiration is life in its multiple facets. She is interested in literature, ranging from poetry to folk tales, from all over the world and from every era. Luisa won a third prize in the inaugural Proverse Poetry Prize competition and her poems have appeared in each of the Proverse Poetry Prize *Mingled Voices* Anthologies.

SIMON THAM is currently an English language and teaching consultant. Before his retirement, he was an English Language and Literature teacher, teacher trainer and Principal Inspector of English in the Hong Kong Government Education Bureau. He is an experienced speech and drama adjudicator and still frequently conducts talks and workshops for both primary and secondary English teachers.

EDWARD A. TIESSE recently returned to Washington State after living for several years in the Chicago area. From his home on clear days, he can see Mount Baker and the Canadian Cascades. Living so close to Canada makes it easy to slip across the border when it becomes necessary.

Edward A. Tiesse has many interests. He loves to cook and recently began baking bread which he soon learned is much like writing poetry. That is, the combinations of flour, water and yeast have many variables and so baking is much like trying to find the right word and its place in a line. Edward's poetry has been published in *The Front Porch Review*, *The Sea Letter* and in the Proverse Poetry Prize Anthologies, *Mingled Voices*.

BIBIANA TSANG is an undergraduate student at the University of Hong Kong. One of her poems, 'Lines Written in Spring' is featured in *People, Pandemic & Protest – The KongPoWriMo 2020 Anthology*. As an amateur poet, her other interests include Chinese art history and Romantic poetry which often inspires her poetic works. In 2020, she has been awarded as the winner of the HKUMS Asian Art Essay Prize Competition. She is the founder of the blog Otiose Literatus, where she regularly shares knowledge on art and literature, and occasionally, her poems. She has always been passionate about encouraging those around her to appreciate the liberal arts and to create works of their own. The blog – Otiose Literatus – is her "small but significant attempt to achieve this."

ROGER UREN is an Australian but he has spent over half his adult life in Asia. He has lived in Hong Kong for thirteen years, in Beijing for four years, as well as lengthy periods of time in Malaysia, India and Taiwan. He worked as an Australian diplomat and public servant from 1974 until 2001, and then served as Vice President of Phoenix Satellite Television in Hong Kong for twelve years. He speaks both Mandarin Chinese and Bahasa Indonesian, which he used when he was working at the Australian High Commission in Kuala Lumpur. He has a long history of involvement with literature, and has written books on Chinese erotic art, on the life of the long-time chief of the Chinese Communist secret service, as well as a novel set in 1980s Beijing and a collection of poetry that he wrote from the 1960s through to the 2000s. He notes that human society has many problems and one of the themes of his recent poetry is how mankind needs to connect different societies and counter the way that egomania tends to influence many global leaders.

DEEPA VANJANI, PHD, heads the English Department in a college in the cleanest city of India, Indore. She has a teaching career spanning 25 years, in which she has published and presented research papers, conducted and participated in workshops, been invited as resource person, key-note speaker, chief guest, and judge in various academic and non academic events.

Apart from academia, Dr Vanjani was a freelance columnist with *Times of India* and *Hindustan Times* for a few years. She intermittently writes features for *Confluence: South Asian Perspectives*, which is published from London.

Her poetry collection, *Shifting Sands*, was published by Proverse in 2016.

She has been recognised for her contribution to media, academia and society through the awards she has received. Deepa runs a literature society called Shabd Shilp, which she founded in 2012. She is an animal lover and works for the welfare of strays.

PETER COE VERBICA grew up on a commercial cattle ranch in Northern California. He obtained a BA and JD from Santa Clara University and an MS from the Massachusetts Institute of Technology. He is married and has four daughters.

KEWAYNE WADLEY is an African-American poet originally from Birmingham, Al and currently resides in Memphis, Tn. His latest work is his self-publishing debut *Listening To Songs At Midnight* and continues to bring the same fun and energy with whatever project he is working on. He also remains very humble & grateful for the opportunity. Previously published & known for his appearance in *The Poetic Bond* series as well as *The Porter Gulch Review*: 36th Edition and the first volume of *Human to Human* from Willowdown Books

VICTORIA WALVIS was born in London and lives in Hong Kong where she teaches English. She is an enthusiastic member of the Peel Street Poets, and organises weekly free creative writing workshops for adults. She was longlisted for the National Poetry Competition in 2019 and shortlisted for The York Poetry Prize in 2020. She is currently working on her first collection of poems.

ANSON HONGHUA WANG, PhD, is an Assistant Professor in Translation. Her research interests are interpreter and translator training, gender and translation and second language acquisition. She is a practicing translator and interpreter. Besides research, she has a wide range of interests including reading, watching movies and hiking. She has been serving as Executive Committee Member of the Hong Kong Association of University Women since 2013. She is also a member of the International Association for Translation and Intercultural Studies.

GEORGE WATT has held teaching, research and administrative positions at universities in Australia, USA, Japan and Macau. He took up the writing of poetry late in life, graduating in creative writing from the University of Edinburgh in Scotland. His first full-length collection of poetry, *Sandpaper Swimming*, has recently been published by Flying Island Books.

MICHAEL WITTS has been writing poetry for more than four decades. Selected early work was published in three volumes: 'Sirens', 'South' and 'Dumb Music'. He was a founding editor of DODO magazine.

Michael was born in Cardiff in 1953 and moved to Australia at the age of five. He studied Arts and Law at Sydney University. He lives in Sydney with his wife Caroline and their daughter. He has three older children and two grandchildren. As well as writing poetry, Michael is a solicitor working in wills and estates.

ZUO FEI (昨 非), resident of Beijing and university English teacher, runs a poetry blog that introduces foreign poetry to Chinese readers. She is an editor and translator of the Spittoon

Literary Magazine, and the featured poet of Spittoon Monthly in May 2020: https://spittooncollective.com/the-poetry-of-zuo-fei/

THE EDITORS

VERNER BICKLEY was born in the North-West of England, and educated there, in Wales and London, and has lived in Asian and Pacific countries for over fifty years.

He has been scholar, teacher, manager, broadcaster, stage and film actor and cultural diplomat in a life often enlivened by music and song, dance and entertainment.

Verner's many scholarly articles and book publications are mainly on educational and cross-cultural topics. He has however also published two volumes of memoirs: *Footfalls Echo in the Memory* and *Steps To Paradise And Beyond*. His five-book graded poetry anthology, *Poems to Enjoy*, has been popular since the 1960s. These now benefit from accompanying recordings of all poems in the texts (read mostly by himself, but some by his wife, Gillian), as well as from teaching and performance notes. He is a member of the United Kingdom Society of Authors.

With his wife, Gillian, Verner Bickley is joint-publisher of Proverse Hong Kong and co-founder of the Proverse Prize and the Proverse Poetry Prize.

Verner was a naval officer in pre-independent Sri Lanka and India. He served in the Colonial Education Service in Singapore and, later, as a British Council officer in post-independence Burma, in Indonesia and Japan. In Hawaii from 1971 to 1981, he served as the Director and for a period Chairman of Directors of the Culture Learning Institute at the East-West Center, established by the US Congress in Hawaii in 1960 and functioning as a US-based institution for public diplomacy with international governance, staffing, students and Fellows.

From 1972 to 1980, Verner led a small team of anthropologists, cross-cultural psychologists and linguists, focusing on the different ways in which individuals and whole societies cope in bicultural and multicultural contexts and how they address problems presented by different cultural norms. Among many interesting projects, his Institute provided for the pioneering voyage of the canoe, *Hōküle'a*, from Hawaii to Tahiti, disproving the theories of Thor Heyerdahl.

Verner was instrumental in bringing to conferences in Honolulu writers who included Guy Amirthanayagam, Leon

Edel, Vincent Eri, Nissim Ezekial, Reuel Denney, Janet Frame, Allen Ginsberg, Syd Harrex, Thomas Keneally, Maxine Hong-Kingston, Arun Kolatkhar, Ananda Murthy, Kenzaburo Oe, Kushwant Singh, Kamala Markandaya, R.K. Narayan, A.K. Ramanajuan, E.R. Sarachchandra, Wole Soyinka and Albert Wendt.

After leaving Hawaii, and while in Saudia Arabia for a two-year assignment with the national airline, Saudia, Verner was responsible for a multi-national staff of 100 persons, mainly, but not exclusively, in Jeddah and Riyadh.

In 1983, Verner was appointed founding director of the Institute of Language in Education in Hong Kong and held that post until 1992. During that period, he created and led annual International conferences on Applied Linguistics and founded and directed the journal, the ILEJ.

Refusing to retire, Verner continues to live in Hong Kong where he writes and publishes on a variety of topics. He was founding Chairman of the English-Speaking Union (Hong Kong) and continued as Chairman of the Executive Committee for sixteen years. He recently passed this responsibility over to a new chairman, but in his capacity as Chairman Emeritus continues with his own portfolio of tasks. As Chairman, he traveled for many years to the Mainland of China to join other judges of the national Public-Speaking Competition organised by national media. He was an adjudicator for the Hong Kong Schools Music and Speech Association's annual Speech Festival for many years and for a while was Representative in Hong Kong for Trinity College London.

Verner Bickley's experiences have created in him an interest in cross-cultural experiences and attitudes and in a desire to communicate what he has learnt. Through his memoirs as well as his personal contacts, he hopes not only to interest others, but to encourage them to build on their own desire to learn about and empathise with other cultures.

THE EDITORS

GILLIAN BICKLEY, born and educated in the United Kingdom, has lived mostly in Hong Kong since 1970. She has been a member of the Society of Authors in the United Kingdom since her school days.

Her poetry collections include *For the Record and other Poems of Hong Kong, Moving House and other Poems from Hong Kong, Sightings: a collection of poetry, China Suite and other Poems, Perceptions*, and *Grandfather's Robin*. Selections from these collections have been published bilingually: in the English-Romanian *Poems/Poeme* (Romanian translation by Carolina Ilica and Dumitru M. Ion) and the English-Italian, *Avvistamenti, pensieri e sentimenti* (Italian translation by Luisa Ternau). Two collections – *Moving House* and *For the Record* – have also been published in Chinese; individual poems have been published in Arabic, Catalan, Chinese, Czech, French, German, Romanian, Turkish and other languages. *Over the Years* (2017) is a selection from her previously published work, selected by Verner Bickley. In 2014, she was awarded the "Grand Prix Orient-Occident Des Arts" at the 18th International Festival, "Curtea de Argeş Poetry Nights", held in Romania. Gillian Bickley is one of the Hong Kong poets discussed in Agnes S. L. Lam's study, *Becoming poets: The Asian English Experience*.

Gillian has written or edited several non-fiction books in different fields: *The Golden Needle: The Biography of Frederick Stewart, 1836-1889 (founder of Hong Kong Government Education)*, Hong Kong Baptist University and David C. Lam Institute for East-West Studies, 1997; *Hong Kong Invaded! A '97 Nightmare*, University of Hong Kong Press, Hong Kong, 2001; *The Development of Education in Hong Kong, 1841-1897: as revealed through the Early Education Reports of the Hong Kong Government, 1848-1896*, Proverse Hong Kong, Hong Kong, 2002; *The Stewarts of Bourtreebush*, Centre for Scottish Studies, University of Aberdeen, Scotland, 2003; *A Magistrate's Court in 19th Century Hong Kong: Court in Time*, Proverse Hong Kong, first edition, 2005; second edition, 2009; *The Complete Court Cases of Magistrate Frederick Stewart*, Proverse Hong Kong, 2008; *In Time of War* (in collaboration with Richard Collingwood-

Selby), an edition based on the writings of Henry C.S. Collingwood-Selby (1898-1992), Lieutenant Commander in the Royal Navy, Proverse Hong Kong, 2013, *Through American Eyes: The Journals of George Washington (Farley) Heard (1837-1875)*, Proverse Hong Kong, 2017; *Journeys with a Mission: Travel Journals of The Right Revd George Smith (1815-1871), first Bishop of Victoria, Hong Kong (1849-1865)*, Proverse Hong Kong, 2018.

Five of these fourteen English-language books received publication support from Hong Kong Arts Development Council (HKADC) and four from the Lord Wilson Heritage Trust. The extensive research necessary for seven of the non-fiction works listed was made possible by research grants awarded by the Hong Kong Baptist University and one was supported by a private sponsor.

Dr Bickley was Senior Lecturer / Associate Professor in the Department of English at the Hong Kong Baptist University for twenty-two years. She has been a full-time faculty member at the University of Lagos, Nigeria; the University of Auckland, New Zealand; and at the University of Hong Kong.

For several years, Gillian was an adjudicator at the world-famous Hong Kong Schools Music & Speech Association's annual Speech Festival and has also been a judge for the Budding Poets' Society Hong Kong.

More recently, as co-ordinator of literary activities for the English-Speaking Union Hong Kong, a non-profit registered educational charity, she has led reading appreciation sessions which are open to the community and assists to deliver reading courses at local schools. She has worked with the Gifted Education Section of the Education Bureau to encourage creative writing among students. On a freelance basis, she has taught creative reading / writing courses at the Hong Kong Academy for Gifted Education (HKAGE) and at the University of Hong Kong School for Professional and Continuing Education (HKU SPACE) and been a guest lecturer on poetry at Lingnan University Community College. Her creative reading / writing course at HKU SPACE continues to be offered. In 2016, she managed twenty and hosted seventeen meet-the-author events at a Hong Kong bookshop. On occasion, she accepts invitations to speak at school Reading Festivals and similar.

Following her career in academia, Gillian has become an experienced publisher, project-manager, text editor, and production manager, including of poetry, non-fiction, fiction and academic writing. She has been President of the Hong Kong Association of University Women and has recently stepped aside from her role as Council Member and a Vice-President of the Royal Asiatic Society (Hong Kong).

PROVERSE HONG KONG: AN INTRODUCTION

Together, Gillian and Verner Bickley are the publishers of Proverse Hong Kong, a Hong Kong-based press which publishes both local and international authors, including non-native users of English. They are also co-founders of two annual international literary prizes for work submitted in English: in 2008, they founded the Proverse Prize for unpublished book-length fiction, non-fiction or poetry, and, in 2016, they established the Proverse Poetry Prize (for single poems which may have been previously published in a language other than English). In the case of both prizes, entries are received from around the world.

Beginning in 2007 up to December 2021, Proverse has managed, edited and published about 139 English-language books by Hong Kong and international writers, five Chinese-language books, one English / Chinese and one English / Italian bilingual book. Of the English-language books, about twenty-eight have been awarded publication support by Hong Kong Arts Development Council (HKADC), four by Lord Wilson Heritage Trust and two by the Ride Fund for publication in the Royal Asiatic Society Hong Kong Studies series. One received a publication grant from the Ministry of Culture of the Czech Republic and one received a publication grant from the Ministry of Culture and Tourism of the Republic of Turkey.

Twice a year, from 2009, Proverse organises literary events in Hong Kong, open to the public. New books are launched, writers are introduced and launching authors give brief talks. Announcements are made relating to the current year's Proverse Prize for unpublished fiction, non-fiction or poetry, and the Proverse Poetry Prize (for single short poems); prizes are presented to those winning authors who are present. Edited videos of some of these events are available on Youtube and photos of most of them are available on the Proverse website, proversepublishing.com.

Gillian and Verner work hard to bring authors before the reading public and to encourage reading as well as writing. On four occasions, they have administered Reading Development Grants awarded by the Hong Kong Arts Development Council. In 2016, as implementation of one of these, they arranged twenty meet-the-author sessions, held at a

Hong Kong bookshop. To reach an international audience, edited videos of these talks are available on Youtube.

Of the titles published by Proverse, several have attracted a Preface or advance appreciation from figures of international reputation, most notably perhaps, from Václav Havel (for the English translation of Olga Walló's *Tightrope: A Bohemian Tale*).

Two titles (Peter Gregoire's, *Article 109* and *The Devil You Know*) were best sellers at Dymocks Hong Kong.

The publication by Proverse of the late Sophronia Liu's book, *A Shimmering Sea*, was a major argument in the award to Sophronia of a posthumous PhD at the University of Minnesota.

Other writers published by Proverse have also benefited in their literary careers, a couple of them taking a leadership role in local literary groups.

Gillian's and Verner's own books and all those by other authors published by Proverse, are available internationally as well as locally, including through the Chinese University of Hong Kong Press. There are copies in the British Library and other legal deposit libraries in the United Kingdom, and in the Hong Kong Public Library system, as well as in many university and public libraries world-wide. Books by Australian writers have been deposited in the National Library of Australia and similar deposits are ongoing in other countries.

POETS' NOTES AND COMMENTARIES

[1] **Face Orogeny**. Vinita Agrawal writes, "the lines on our face have a specific name. In other words, wrinkles have monikers. For example, the lines at the outer corners of our eyes, are called crows-feet, the wrinkles around our lips are laugh lines and those between our eyebrows, elevens.

"I've also wondered about Orogeny, the process by which the earth's crust folds into a mountain by lateral compression. I sensed a parallel between the lines on our faces and the processes that deform the Earth's crust.

"Reading these specific terms for facial lines, on Google, prompted me to write something on the subject. The first stanza of the poem makes use of the different phrases to describe these lines. However, what the poem really seeks to do, is to go beyond what is skin deep, beyond what is visible to the deep, hidden space of pain, hurt and grief. It seeks to exfoliate the spaces of pain and touch the experiences that might have caused the lines to appear in the first place."

[2] **A Walk in the Woods**. Joy Al-Sofi writes, "Everyday, when the weather isn't bad, I go for a walk near my house. Very close by, there is a small remnant of rain forest, with a few tiny farms and invasive plants that hug the hillside next to the path. From the path I can see how the foliage changes and some of the species of birds, reptiles, insects and spiders that live there. Unfortunately, there are far fewer of all of them this year. I'd like to think it was because of the later rains, but I have read of a global loss of insect populations.

"I have seen many amazing things and I have learned a great deal about nature and myself each time I go out. I understand that dangers exist for people there, especially if we are not careful, but I have come to understand that the greater danger comes from us to them, than from them to us. I wanted to capture that feeling, along with sharing some of what I was seeing."

³ **From an Autumn Hillside**. Joy Al-Sofi writes, "I was watching a programme that showed beautiful autumn scenes and foliage in China. I imagined I was in China in the autumn.

"I wanted to capture the atmosphere that I get from many of the ancient Chinese poems. I also wanted to reference the idea of a lonely, solitary person who waits, perhaps in vain, while he sees others enjoying themselves. But he is also aware that not all who are on pleasure boats are necessarily happy to be there, given the underlying reality of what the term 'pleasure boats' can reference. This is the idea behind clouds, dancing and weeping.

"In the end, the narrator's wait may seem fruitless but the poem contains a smidgen of hope as we are reminded we are not the first to have passed this way. And the words of the poets remain."

⁴ **Halfway or More?** Joy Al-Sofi writes, "When I look at the state of the world, what I see is a human species that is walking itself over a cliff. This is what we used to falsely claim lemmings did. Turns out we were projecting. I am worried that our species will self-destruct in the not too distant future and take much of the rest of life with us because it seems not enough of us are willing to do what it takes to find the solutions and stop it.

"First, I looked at our closest relatives. Genetically, we are basically equidistant from chimpanzees and bonobos. We have inherited aspects of both. Halfway between those two: but what if we didn't inherit the right halves, or not enough of the right halves? That is the meaning of between "I'll take that," very chimpanzee-like, while "cooperate," including loving the stranger, is very much a bonobo trait.

"Turning from our closest living relatives, I looked back at our ancestral, hominid lineage to see how all the other hominids fared. I saw how long ago this branch of the family tree began, approximately 5 millions years ago, and what names we have called them. I made a list of those extinct hominids and left a space at the diminishing end for us.

"This is not predictive, but a reflection of deep sadness."

[5] **RIP/RAP**. Joy Al-Sofi writes, "The video of a Minneapolis Police officer pressing his knee on George Floyd's neck for more than nine minutes, is an absolute outrage and has become an indelible memory of our time. I needed to express how affected I was and to proclaim that this couldn't be allowed to continue. That led me to write this poem which turned out to be a rap.

"The words are clear and require no further discussion or explanation. We just need to think about them."

[6] **A Perfect Mimic**. Joy Al-Sofi writes, "[This poem] is the result of my more recent nature walks and seeing how perfectly butterflies imitate leaves and flowers. That butterflies do this seemed a no-brainer until I read that new findings in the fossil record show that butterflies are far older than angiosperms (flowering plants).

"That has just stayed in my mind and played with my imagination and led to the conclusion that when we think we know something, we may be as far from what is true as possible. I wanted to capture that feeling of cognitive dissonance, as well as marvel, that I experience every time I see a butterfly and a flowering plant. It is a reminder that we humans, too often, have taken irreversible actions based on faulty understanding."

[7] **Watching Katmai**. Joy Al-Sofi writes, "The internet is a powerful tool which has many wonderful aspects but also some unsavory ones. One of the things it can do best is to connect us to that which really matters, and for me that is nature. But while it does connect us, it is a suspect connection, one that not only can be dropped without leave or notice, it also removes us from what is tangible in nature, leaving us once again in our own heads living in a virtual world that is literally lifeless and where our actions have no consequences. I wanted to capture both the wonders and the pitfalls involved in the way this connection can make us feel. One of these is that after our virtual meal, we are empty and still in need of real food. We need to reconnect with the real world.

"Katmai National Park has a webcam that streams live from Brook Falls, Alaska on Explore.org. In summer, you can watch the bears gather for the salmon feast. There may be many bears there and, unlike most other predators, they rarely chase each other away.

"At the same time, the salmon are fighting the current along with the bears, the gulls and eagles in order to get back to their natal ground which is where they breed, and where they die.

"Even after death, their bodies provide nourishment. They sacrifice themselves for the benefit of the future, not only of their offspring, but other salmon and the entire Pacific-Northwest ecosystem. Pacific salmon present a perfect metaphor for, and symbol of, the circle of life.

"I wanted to express my love for and connection with what I feel is really there, more than just what we are seeing from the false comfort of our distant lives. "

[8] **Word/s.** Joy Al-Sofi writes, "I am, and have been, immersed in, and enmeshed with, words but I have lately become more wary of them. I was a very talkative child and always deeply interested in how words were used, often to cover up and avoid the truth. Whenever I heard someone doing that, I took it as an indictment of the one doing that. Even when very young, I used to call them out, which, as you can imagine, was not always received well. (Nor is it now.)

"Recently I have been questioning language and words themselves. These are our tools but they lend themselves too easily to painting a false picture. Have we used language to distance ourselves from reality and nature especially? I feel we, as a species, are often far too thoughtless in our relationship with words. I felt the need to send a caution."

[9] **A Trip To The Supermarket.** Shikha Bansal writes, "The poem is a reflection on the consumerism that defines society, today. Everything is ours for the asking and supermarkets are bursting with produce from all over the world, in stark contrast to the lives of our ancestors who hunted or picked their food."

[10] **Safe Landing.** Shikha Bansal writes, "I wrote this poem in the first year of the pandemic, when travel had slowed down to a trickle and the sight of a plane had the ability to surprise you.

It is a rumination on the experience and compulsions of travel during Covid, and also on the human race's unthinking exploitation of the planet."

[11] **The Wind.** Shikha Bansal tells us that this poem, "is a result of a walk on a blustery day in Hong Kong. The poem is a homage to one of nature's elements that can be destructive, yet playful and uplifting.'

[12] **Youth.** Andrew Barker writes, " 'Youth' is a testament to and celebration of youthful ambition, endeavor and hard work. The title, theme, and inspiration of the poem come from two novellas, one by Joseph Conrad the other by J. M. Coetzee, both of the name *Youth*, and both dealing with the ability of the young to overcome obstacles, usually through a dogmatic determination fuelled by enthusiasm, energy and belief that things will improve. The poem is the more optimistic if the three works.

" 'Youth' is highly and specifically autobiographical, dealing with the poet's art-inspired intellectual journey from manual laborer to writer; a journey creating an individual so different from the one who started it that the poet sees his former self as an "other", referring to him in the third person. All this is biographically accurate. The poet worked as, was, a bricklayer from the age of fifteen until twenty-one (and his thought-processes and idiolect of that time are reflected in the poem), and currently works as a university lecturer in literature.

"The poet's recollection of his youthful self is initiated by him coming upon a folder of poems painstakingly copied down by his younger self, and his own first attempt at putting thoughts into verse. While acknowledging the deficiencies in that first poem, the poet is grateful for the efforts made by the youth who wrote it, and copied all those poems out. It is the initial effort of that youth–which allowed the poet to be the person he now is as he looks back at the person he was. And it is the hope-inspired energy of that youth which the poet, in awe of the boy's achievement, doubts he could still replicate.
I think many of us often have a tendency to regard our youthful naivety with a self-protective disdain. We may feel we are better people now through being worse people then. This may

be helpful, and may be true, but the poem hopes to show that it is worth acknowledging more positively certain attributes we had when young and which we may have lost in the journey launched by that person we once were."

[13] **Panhandler's Lullaby.** Gary Beaumier writes, "So often driving along the off ramp of the freeway there are the homeless begging. One particular man I saw wore a look of such desperation and I couldn't help but think of my own son who was going through a difficult time. It is so easy to suppose that these souls have no connection to us and yet for a simple tweak in our lives, like the trauma of wartime experiences, we could so easily be amongst these discarded humans."

[14] **The anger of the frozen, dying.** Alan Bern writes, '[This poem] has many referents and derivations, most of which have travelled to and from my life's experiences. For better and worse, death surrounds us: it is fact. Some accept this; many others do not. What is not at all set is how we shall die, our dying, nor how we may react to this fact and to the dying process. In this poem I create a voice and character from a number of people I have known. This character is responding to parts of the reality of death and to the dying process: simultaneously she cannot believe that she still lives, nor that she will die soon … soon, certainly a relative term. When I was a young adult I had a very ill and permanently damaged family member. Some who knew her thought she would have been better off dead. On the other hand, in speaking of her, a very wise adult in my life, a medical doctor and the father of one of my oldest friends, told me that he did not think that people should die before their time. He was not an obviously religious man, and I have never been quite sure what he meant by 'their time,' but he seemed to believe that people should live as long as they could, as long as possible. This surprised me, still surprises me thirty years after his own death from cancer. I do believe that life is of inestimable value, is even sacred. And I tend to believe that we only have one time alive though of this I am not certain. How to respond to these ambivalences, uncertainties, paradoxes, con-fusions. With anger perhaps? In my poem anger reigns in many of its aspects. Anger is an

uncomfortable emotion for so many of us, this writer included. I offer this poem as one response.

[15] **Avian Villanelle.** Thea Biesheuvel writes, "The 'avian' reference is, of course, to birds. They are entirely free to zoom through the air; they can change their environment with just a few flaps of their wings.

"I grew up during World War II in the Netherlands. We were a country with occupational forces stationed everywhere. *Oh, to be a bird on the wing at times*, I thought, *to fly away to freedom*.

"The reason birds appeal to me in poetry is because the imagery can also make the words and phrases soar.
Sometimes birds just sit and wait and see. They can outfox a snake eyeing them from below. Then, suddenly there'll be a flash of feathers. These tendencies describe my nature perfectly.

"So, for me, the reason the Villanelle is 'the' structure for such poetry is that there is no need for a narrative. The form circles around and around, refusing to go forward in any linear development. It suggests powerful recurrences of mood, emotion and memory.

"The Villanelle repeats sounds time and time again. Lines can also be repeated.

"The repeated sounds and lines become a repudiation of forward movement and of time, but finally offer some dissolution or resolution.

"The poem so becomes a series of retrieved feelings and images, just like those that occurred in my childhood, providing food for thought."

[16] **The shielder, the shielded.** Liam Blackford writes, " 'The shielder, the shielded' is a poem with six stanzas, each stanza with six lines, each line with six syllables. The poem depicts two figures, not gendered, who speak to each other in turn: one speaks first, then the second. The figures stand in grotesque disproportion to each other: the first gigantic, the second tiny. Each figure bemoans their relationship to the other, with emotions swerving from fondness and warmth to scorn and contempt. Each figure speaks only as much as the other, and

each figure's words mirror the other. With this balanced and bifurcated structure, the poem has the energy of a swinging pendulum which we imagine swinging back and forth even after the poem ends. The poem articulates the complexity and ambivalence of human intimacy, in which power and sensitivity ebb and flow and in which euphoric fantasy is interrupted by painful reality."

[17] **Palace Of Winds, Jaipur.** Maria Elena Blanco writes, "This poem was conceived during a trip to India in 2010, when I visited several cities in that country after attending a poetry festival in Mysore. I was inspired to write a series of poems as a result of different incidents and experiences I had in each of those cities, which eventually formed a group of poetic texts I informally collected under the title 'Horror vacui', an expression meaning literally 'fear of the void'. This denomination was suggested to me by the sharp contrast between the proliferation of very strong material, sensory, images of the daily life, customs and history, including massive architecture, that India offered to the mind and eye, which gave a raw sense of the mortal human condition, on the one hand, and the ineffable spirituality of its multiple religious cults, often characterized by an ascetic or mystical bent, on the other. Somehow, under all that visual exuberance there was a desire for annihilation – hence the importance of fire in that culture – in a spiritual dimension paradoxically materialized in renouncement and, ultimately, death. There was a double life, an outward ritual and an intimate undoing, a capitulation to dire tradition and, at the same time, a joyful liberation through sheer spirit and power of mind.

"In 'Palace of the Winds, Jaipur', the magnificent, profusely decorated edifice offered to the sight of tourists is shown as what it really was: an empty front which hid the only windows to the outside world, along a series of stairs and passageways, that allowed the recluse wives of the maharaja to fleetingly escape the slavery of (male) polygamous wedlock and to fantasize about other, more satisfying pleasures. Beyond that façade there is a huge void, an open but enclosed courtyard adjacent to what were, in a different, recessed building, the women's quarters, designed for their feminine and motherly labours. The poem describes the inner reality of the 'palace' and of the women who inhabited it, and warns the unsuspecting tourist about the often-deceptive and ambiguous surface of words and places."

[18] **The Tusk.** Gavin Bourke writes, "The story of this poem ... that my father-in-law was cleaning out his garage a few months ago and we happened to be visiting. He took a carved tusk from the boot of a car and asked me if I would like it. I didn't really know what it was apart from the fact that it was a tusk shape and heavy to lift. I took it home and cleaned it with a small brush and some solution. The colour went from a dark brown to a bright yellow within an hour or two and I realised that the whole of one side of the tusk was carved with the most beautiful imagery. Part of me was uncomfortable with the tusk being what it is but another part of me was fascinated by the artwork and craftsmanship which is exquisite. I wondered who would likely have carved it. I did some research into the tusk and discovered it is not ivory but most likely a mixture of bone and a synthetic substance called cellulose. This type of sculpture is called a chryselephantine sculpture and the type of carving or artwork is called scrimshaw artwork. It is a soaring sequence of Chinese historical images including fans, emperors, flags, figures and scenes which look very much Chinese in content. My father-in-law told me a door-to-door salesman sold it to him approximately fifty years ago and that he had kept it since. They are quite rare with few going up for auction as they are not so valuable or those that are would perhaps be even rarer. I was so fascinated by all of this that I decided to write a poem about it which would be suitable and specific to this particular competition and I'm so glad it has been awarded a place as I am very proud of it and I learned a lot about Chinese culture and history and about myself in its creation. Currently the bone tusk is in my living room on top of a book-shelf where it continues to inspire my writing."

[19] **One of Those Linoleum Days.** Lawrence Bridges writes, "I've always liked the way this poem pushes the language forward. 'LINOLEUM DAYS' is code for a mood where childhood memories volatilize: a cheek pressed to a linoleum

floor examining bread crumbs, the buckling yellow countertop of a cheap cabin in the mountains, or the chemical smell of linoleum mixed with debilitatingly hot smoggy days in the San Fernando Valley in Los Angeles. It's a mood of anxiety and nausea with the hope the next day comes healed of headache, neuralgia ennui, and hopelessness. 'Down under, a readiness to face facts, and return the broken mind to its golden home.' "

[20] **Acute psychosis/In Murakami novels world.** Lina Buividavičiūtė writes, "One of the most important themes of my poetry is mental illnesses/disorders. I want to integrate both personal experience and art contexts in my poetry. This is what I do in 'Acute psychosis/In Murakami novels world' poem. I try to connect my understanding of a very difficult psychological state, serious mental illness and to give some background of it based on literature – Murakami's novels."

[21] **Cotard delusion.** Lina Buividavičiūtė explains, "Cotard's delusion, also known as walking corpse syndrome or Cotard's syndrome, is a rare mental disorder in which the affected person holds the delusional belief that they are dead, do not exist, are putrefying, or have lost their blood or internal organs (Berrios G.E.; Luque R. (1995). 'Cotard's delusion or syndrome?'.*Comprehensive Psychiatry*. 36 (3): 218–223)

[22] **Leda Syndrome.** Lina Buividavičiūtė writes, "Mythology and literature – so intertextuality – are very important in this poem. I wanted to take the myth of Leda and the Greek god Zeus and W. B. Yeats' famous poem, 'Leda and the Swan' and to write my own modern poetical interpretation of these contexts. Also, some feminist discourse is important in my poem."

[23] **On Devils and Obsessive-Compulsive Disorder.** Lina Buividavičiūtė writes, " 'On Devils and Obsessive-Compulsive Disorder' is one of the most autobiographical poems I have ever written. I have faced obsessive-compulsive disorder – all these strange annoying 'bad' thoughts – and have tried to find a deep understanding of it – where did it come from, what experience, archetypes and other structures of my psyche have

had an impact leading to my disorder? In doing this, I thought about my grandmother's stories and tried to think about obsessions and 'evil' more widely."

[24] **Shadows of Mothers.** Lina Buividavičiūtė writes, "Usually, we think about the concept of 'mother' in positive way. I wanted to emphasise the other side, the darkness of the 'mother' archetype. I tried to find depth of this concept, to highlight trans-generative traumas."

[25] **Stendhal's syndrome.** Lina Buividavičiūtė explains, "Stendhal's syndrome or Florence syndrome is a psychosomatic condition involving rapid heartbeat, fainting, confusion and even hallucinations, allegedly occurring when individuals become exposed to objects, artworks, or phenomena of great beauty."

[26] **XS.** Lina Buividavičiūtė writes, "This is one of the darkest poems I have ever written. I wanted to write 'XS' for all those who have faced eating disorders. This poem doesn't promise salvation but talks about all the difficulties, confusion and darkness which eating disorders bring. I wanted to emphasize deep traumas – the impact of childhood and relationships among family members – to understand better people suffering from eating disorders."

[27] **A Social Distance.** Vincent Casaregola writes, "During the 2020-2021 Academic Year, at the height of the COVID pandemic, I would go to my office in the Humanities Building on our campus. Sometimes I did this during the day, but mostly at night, when fewer people were present. I was teaching through distance methods, both synchronous and asynchronous. In my office at night, I would work on my computer for several hours. It was very quiet, and it seemed almost ghostly, but I knew others were also in the building because I could hear a door shut occasionally or the elevator rising and lowering with a passenger. Sometimes, I heard footsteps, and donning my mask, I would peek out the office door to see, but no one remained. The sound of footsteps was already fading as it moved around the corner. The images of the poem are

accurate descriptions of the place and the time, including the soiled microwave and the missing soap. Sometimes, I began to recall the number of offices that were not just empty for a time but whose occupants had died recently. We were all encouraged to keep a social distance, and the distances I experienced, between me and the invisible others in the building, and between me and those who had died, informed the tone and texture of the poem. The sound of air moving through the pipes and vents was like a spirit song, a voice of the dead, or a chant in an unknown, ancient language. Most buildings are filled with ghosts but are too crowded with the living for us to notice. In times of greater isolation, however, we may hear their subtle voices, a trick of memory and a trick of fate."

Editors' note: "Hollywood Squares" is an American game-show in which two contestants compete in a game of tic-tac-toe win cash and prizes.

[28] **The Reptilian.** Kwan Ee Chan, Tom, writes, "[This poem] was originally written as a overview of life, about the fragility of life itself and the resistance of living. The subject, therefore, was supposed to be *human*. So I was surprised, as I was writing the poem, I realised how similar it is between a person and a reptile – how we are born fragile, innocent, and eager; then as we live on, we learn to put on a shield of amour and we keep to ourselves 'for survival' – that's what we tell ourselves. But at the end of the path, we're scared to be alone, knowing that death is solitary, and we'll all end up in a fridge one day. So we say that reptiles are cold-blooded and unsettling… but how about us?"

[29] **A Prayer for my Daughter** (*unentered poem*). Margaret Clarke writes, "The occasion was an urgent mission to Turkey where my daughter was dangerously ill. I shall never forget the kindness and care shown to both of us by staff and patients at the hospital where she was treated."

[30] **The Yew Hedge** (*unentered poem*). Margaret Clarke writes, "Much labour went into the creation of that hedge! More

labour went into nursing it through those early weeks during a warm summer: I remember staggering up and down a field with buckets of water morn and eve. Then the wildlife moved in: badger to dig up the roots; muntjac to push through it. Even now, when we can admire a green wall, Muntjac still try to push through. Being older now, I tend to live and let live."

[31] **Butterfly in the Snow.** William Leo Coakley writes, "There are too many homeless men and women living in the streets of New York (and elsewhere in the world), many of them addicts or mentally ill. But last winter during the worst of the pandemic I noticed one big and strong and clean man in his fifties gathering newspapers left over by the newsagents, I presumed for a makeshift mattress. When I offered him money for food, he refused, saying he didn't believe in money.

"As I talked with him later, he was very much clear-headed and intelligent and knew more about the world than I do – he had been reading those papers. He told me he had lived in the streets of Japan for twenty years before he came to New York ten years ago.

"He had a daughter and a father still alive who is an Episcopalian minister but he had long ago left al that behind.

"When he found out I was a poet, he said he had written a poem and he recited one in the Japanese haiku form which was better than most of what I read in the magazines. But I couldn't remember the whole poem, only the last line: 'a butterfly in the snow' and he couldn't either when I asked him again. So I had to retrieve it somehow in this poem honouring him.

"I am sad that I have not seen him this winter – I can only hope he has removed to China."

[32] **Complicated.** Audrey Colasanti writes, "This poem started as a tribute to my son, Lou, who has had five open-heart surgeries to repair a faulty heart valve." Then the poem changed and took a different form, "each stanza 'seemingly' unrelated to the one before it, while in fact, they are all about love. Love can be so complicated and messy, misunderstood."

[33] **Displaced**. Audrey Colasanti writes, "I wrote this poem while waiting for a flight out of Chicago's O'Hare Airport. I saw this young boy with his father and grandmother. They looked so scared and lost."

Editors' note: TSA (The Transportation Security Administration): an agency of the U.S. Department of Homeland Security that has authority over the security of the traveling public in the United States.
Payless: an international discount footwear chain.

[34] **Freeze Frame**. Audrey Colasanti writes, "I have always been an anxious person...afraid of heights, afraid of enclosed spaces, afraid of walking on ice. I know my fears are irrational and ruin many fun moments. 'Freeze Frame' is a brief glimpse into my thought process as I walk across what-I-believe to be thin ice, when in fact, it is quite thick and safe."

[35] **Gig at the Picnic**. Audren Colasanti writes, "I wrote this after going to our local farmers' market and observing all the 'whiteness' in the crowd. A black band was playing funky R&B to the all-white crowd, which seemed so awkward and shameful to me. Shameful, in that this was clearly a place that only white people could afford to shop (for fresh organic foods), while the blacks entertained us. This was also after the George Floyd incident, which occurred in my city, Minneapolis, Minnesota, USA."

[36] **Meat**. Audrey Colasanti writes, "Sadly, this poem is about someone I know who was obviously struck in the face by her husband (who refused to acknowledge his abuse)."

[37] **Oh Mother**. Audrey Colasanti writes, "My mother was a child of The Depression and a strict, authoritarian upbringing. She struggled to find joy and an easy laughter. She struggled to relax and allow herself personal comforts. In my memories, she spent much of the time with her "head bent down", not making eye contact, seemingly consumed by her own deep worries and woes. Naturally, this was sad for me and I still struggle to

figure out what all of her hidden demons were....although I can guess..."

Editors' note: "satyres en atlante": a group of statues on display in the Louvre Museum in Paris.

[38] **As the Shield Lifted**. Suzanne Cottrell writes, "In writing, I often draw inspiration from my surroundings, especially nature. My sheltering at home during the Covid pandemic resembled the confinement of a queen bee to her hive. Initially, I was content being a homebody, preferring to spend time at home rather than risk exposure to the Covid virus by participating in activities within the community. I cared for my family like a queen bee cares for her colony. Technology provided temporary relief, enabling me to communicate with others. However, prolonged social, physical isolation impacted the mood and tone of my writing, which became more macabre (grim, upsetting, and disheartening). As an observer and lover of nature, I turned to nature to help lift my spirits, renew my creativity, and give me hope. When faced with adversity, we can learn from nature if we'll take the time to stop, watch, and listen."

[39] **Absolute Abyss,** Alecia Dantico writes, "describes the state of despair that the writer falls into following a domestic violence incident that occurred on her honeymoon. The poem recounts her loss of innocence and the abyss of despair into which she finds herself as she tries to process and understand the horror of abuse. Writing and the ordered realm of formal poetry represents the writer's attempt to create an alternate universe where structure and sense, rather than chaos, reign."

[40] **When Manny Pacquiao sprained**. Lawdenmarc Decamora writes, "Poetry is the art of practicing psychogeography on the page. It's taking pleasure in the ludic performances of words, ideas, or language as a whole. Precisely, I used to derive poetry here from the perspective of the suburban neighbourhood, which is my own vision of the spectacle of words in delirium, of gossips which aestheticize fragmented ideas, as well as line breaks only to be recontextualized and reconstructed by

dream(s). The poem's enjambed title, 'When Manny Pacquiao sprained,' has this purpose to explore how memory like a crowded toda terminal is reconstructed through the articulation of the forgotten rituals and traditions, such as going to church on Sundays or patronizing a sports icon, as it were, as a symbolic means to escape reality if not poverty. It's obvious that I play around and uncover the lyrical message as a way to detail the binary truth most Filipinos encounter: fandom and marginality. On this note, music plays an effective role of spatializing and exploring memory, not to mention the deliberate use of couplets to magnify binarism once and for all."

Manny Pacquiao: Filipino politician and former professional boxer.
Toda terminals: A common place or town terminal where Philippine tricycles (or *trikes*) are used as service vehicles.

[41] **Aubade.** Neil Douglas explains that, " 'aubade' is a French word meaning 'dawn serenade' but this poem is perhaps more of a dawn lament for lost love and was written in response to a workshop featuring the poems of W.H. Auden."

[42] **Le chat.** Neil Douglas writes that this poem was written in a workshop based around a poem of the same name by Charles Baudelaire.

[43] **Lips**. Neil Douglas writes that this poem, "moves from consideration of anatomical function to urgent unbalanced erotic obsession in a very compressed form."

[44] **Mrs Charybdis.** Neil Douglas writes that his poem, "takes Homeric legend into suburban London during Lockdown. The mythical monsters are neighbours living on opposite sides of the street and Mr Charybdis has disappeared. Has he become stuck 'between a rock and a hard place'? Scylla might know."

[45] **Sylvia calls Time.** Neil Douglas writes that this poem, "was written on the emergence from Lockdown. On the surface it is about a publican calling last orders in a London bar on a Friday

night. However, the name Sylvia is derived from the Latin word for forest and could be taken to mean the spirit of the wood. A 'punter' in vernacular British means a customer but is also a gambler. Maybe Mankind is gambling with the natural environment and we are in the last chance saloon?"

[46] **The anatomy of her neck.** Neil Douglas explains that this is, "an ekphrastic piece (a poem based on a work of art) inspired by the anatomical drawings of Leonardo Da Vinci and the tension between beauty and function. The meter of the poem is slightly off pentameter with some end rhyme, half rhyme and repetition which seeks to accentuate the tension but aid flow when read aloud."

[47] **My house is a superhero.** A.D. Elliott writes, "This poem was written during a strict lockdown for COVID 19 in the UK. It meant that people were not allowed out of their houses for more than an hour a day. We were to stay indoors to keep safe. It was as if our house were shielding us or protecting us from the COVID pandemic. My poem draws on the theme of the superhero using well known hero references from films and comic culture to make comparisons between our simple house and that of a superhero, as our house really was keeping us safe at this time."

[48] **Twineham.** DW Evans writes, "The poem takes its name from the Mid-Sussex village of Twineham – a small affair of perhaps a hundred dwellings, a school and of course the church which is the subject of the piece. I visited St Peters just as Covid restrictions were lifting in England, during that week in June 2020 when places of worship could unlock – although the key-keeper for this church wasn't disposed to open it.

"The church dates from the early 16th century and is appropriately constructed from small red Tudor bricks and tiled with hefty Horsham stone slabs. Given that the church was locked, there was little else to do but examine the graveyard and in doing so I gathered the impression of a place of guarded inclusion. For example the Quaker or nonconformist portion of the graveyard is factual. Unable to secure burial rights in the area, St Peters 'rented' out a corner of the field for a peppercorn rent.

"On the theme of the excluded included, especially in times of social distancing, the squint or grill on the rear door of the church seemed especially poignant. It should be noted here that I can find no corroboration that this was an actual squint or hagioscope, other than what I was told by a person tending a grave. Squints are usually generous peek holes set aslant and cut into the fabric of the building, allowing the *diseased* a chance to watch a ritual they could no longer participate in. The St Peter squint, however, is more of window cut into the door, shuttered in the speakeasy sense and covered by an iron grill.

"While I appreciate there are hundreds of poems set in graveyards, there was something optimistic about Twineham's Church of St Peter. Outsiders were included here – well as much as they could be, considering the legal constraints placed on the control of contagion and the limited freedoms placed on some faiths at the time."

[49] **Daisy In Chains.** Adele Evershed writes, "[This poem] was written in response to the abduction and murder of Sarah Everard in March. She had been walking home from a friend's house in Clapham, London, about 9 pm. Sarah did all the things women are recommended to do to make themselves safe; she walked well-lit streets and spoke to her boyfriend on the phone, but she never made it home. Her body was found in a wooded area in Kent. A serving police officer Wayne Couzens pleaded guilty to her murder. There were vigils across Britain, and women shared their experiences of being harassed on streets and public transport and demanded more protection. I wrote my poem in the form of a Bop, which the Academy of American Poets defines as 'a form of poetic argument consisting of three stanzas, each stanza followed by a repeated line'. The repeated line 'Pile the stones around the hawthorn to stop the cows from coming' is taken from the tradition in Ireland where farmers would pile boulders around hawthorn trees; the trees were believed to be fairy trees and the stones would stop them from being damaged.

"I chose daisies because of their association with innocence and the game 'He loves me, He loves me not'. The destruction of something beautiful to decide if a man cares was, I felt, the perfect image for a poem that deals with violence against women.

"The #MeToo movement had heartened me somewhat. Being a young woman in the 1980s, I had to deal with attention from men, which was really sexual harassment, and I am so glad my daughter has the tools to recognize this behavior and call it out. But as the Sarah Everard case has shown, there is still so much more that needs to be done until women can feel safe. Women must force Governments to do more, and we should not be expected to trade our freedom for safety. Why should we have to change our behavior, not go out at night, dress a certain way, etc., to avoid the risk of harassment or violence? Women need men to change their behavior, and maybe they could start by asking what they could do to help."

[50] **Protection Spells (Shielding).** Daniela Fischerová writes, "Perhaps none of my poems have such a clear and intelligible back-story as this one. I was on a Buddhist meditation course. I was sitting in a mountain summer meadow, observing my mind. My mind is usually boringly still, but that day it was overwhelmed by a sense of futility. My emotional bottom is not anger, fear or sadness, it is the awareness of absolute meaningless-ness. Life seemed to me to be a stumble without purpose and I felt incredibly sorry for all of us living creatures who wander from nothingness to nothingness: there is no reason. I sat motionless, with only tears streaming down until they wet my summer blouse. My mind desperately searched for some argument as to why we should even bother to be here, and a very clear image of blueberries and cream and sugar emerged. Yes, they're good. Oh, so good. Perhaps they alone are worth enduring the hardships of existence for. And at the same time I knew what a ridiculous gimmick it was, a bowl of blueberries couldn't justify the bottomless suffering of the world. Still, it was the only voice that voted in favor of life.
" I told the story at home and for the next Christmas my daughter gave me blueberry compote, a bag of sugar and a bottle of cream."

[51] **Redshirt Daddy.** Casey Hampton writes, "The term 'Redshirt' most often refers to characters from the original Star Trek television series who wore red Starfleet uniforms, were perceived as being expendable, and who often disappeared or died tragically on away missions. Such characters usually had names, but this was about all the audience would know about them."

She adds, " 'Wagon Train to the stars' was part of creator Gene Roddenberry's pitch for the original Star Trek, as 'Wagon Train' was a popular television Western which Roddenberry wanted to suggest his Star Trek could mirror in popularity.

"The phrase 'Steady as she goes,' was a common phrase and command given by Captain Kirk, and it means, 'Carry on.' "

[52] **Lost Cities.** R. J. Keeler writes, "The "back story" for my poem is pretty simple. Somehow, somewhere, I came across a reference to Alan Weisman's book *World Without Us*. I located a copy in my local library and was fascinated by it. After finishing the book and after a short time to mull it over, I came up with the concept for the poem. The poem went through sixteen revisions up to the point I submitted it to the International Proverse Poetry Prize."

[53] **Maginot line.** Christos Koukis gives the following notes:
1. a line of fortifications built by France to defend its border with Germany prior to World War II; it
proved ineffective against the German invasion
2. any line of defence in which blind confidence is placed.

[54] **Ode to Access.** Lynda Lambert writes, "This poem began to form in my thoughts as I was denied access to my G-mail account. I wanted to respond to an essay written by Alice Massa, but could not get into my mail. In this poem which I constructed from the text of the mail I wanted to send, I speak of the struggles I sometimes have with adaptive technology for the blind. As a visually impaired poet, I depend on technology to do many things in my personal and professional life. As I became aware of the challenge in trying to get into my account, I also thought of the complexity of using pronouns. I wrote it in

the form of poetry. I needed a good cup of coffee to settle my thoughts."

55 Ancient Texts. Lynda McKinney Lambert writes, "In my list of 'Poems in Progress,' I wrote the word, 'Ancient.' Often, my poems begin when one word enters into my consciousness. I write it down; I wait for more clarity on the word and eventually, I begin to create the poem. In this poem, I mingle the names of God, and historical context, with my own thoughts and actions as I write. The Abecedarian format gave me a good structure on which I could build this poem as I visit past, present and future landscapes and stories. "

56 Daily Awakenings. Lynda McKinney Lambert writes, "Sometimes it takes many years for me to complete a poem. I have to wait until I have lived through some circumstances in life so that I can see the bigger picture of the idea I had initially. I never rush my poems; I wait on them to guide me in the process of creation.

"This poem began to take form in 1992. I wrote down some fragments while observing the behavior of a person I knew. I was frustrated, angry and homesick at this time because I was living in California but I wanted to go back home with my family in Pennsylvania. I jotted down the pieces of this poem at that time.

"After I sketched out my thoughts in 1992, I did not return to them until 2021.

"I looked through my poetry archives. When I read the fragments, they merged with my present observations of my husband and his daily challenges. I saw so many parallels with the things I was thinking about so long ago. My husband is in remission from Acute Myeloid Leukemia since 2014. He suffered through months of terrifying treatments and a stem cell transplant that year. All of these left impressions in his mind that he deals with daily.

"I merged attributes of dementia with characteristics of two men to create this poem."

57 Letter to Jack Frost. Lynda McKinney Lambert writes, "Winter is my favorite season; Jack Frost is always associated with the attributes of winter. My poetic letter addresses all of the complaints I hear from people who dislike winter. As I wrote the poem, I envisioned those negative statements with a bit of humor. I addressed each one in my letter to the fictional character who symbolizes the winter season. I chose the Pi format because it is in March, and where I live, the weather is usually brutal in March. Yet, this is the time when local residents are complaining the loudest about winter weather."

[58] **Viewing Red Falls.** Lynda McKinney Lambert writes, "Akiko Kotani is a fiber artist who lives in Florida. She is a retired professor of fine art and I studied with her during my years at Slippery Rock University as I worked to earn my BFA Degree in painting. She mentored me and gave me a passion for fiber art. Recently, I saw photos of her latest work at an art gallery. This poem is the response I wrote while viewing a photo of her standing beside her powerful sculpture of fiber that has the feeling of a red waterfall plunging from the ceiling of the gallery.

"Art and artists are the focus and theme for my poetry and non-fiction essays. I honor and celebrate the artists and their work in my writing. Akiko Kotani was a major influence in my creative life during my academic studies and remains so to this day."

[59] **Warm Thanks.** Lynda McKinney Lambert writes, "I save letters and notes that are sent to me by other artists and writers who are friends. For this poem, the letter was an e-mail from Milwaukee, Wisconsin – from Alice Jane-Marie Massa. Like me, Alice is a retired English teacher and is blind. We met some years ago when I joined a writer's organization, 'Behind Our Eyes.' We have served together on committees, the group's board, and we formed a deep friendship through our mutual love of poetry.

"For this poem, I used her note and reformulated it into a 'found poem.'

"She labelled her letter to me as 'Warm Thanks.' It was the perfect feeling for our friendship and our love of poetry and English literature.

"This found poem is a continuation of my interest in honoring and recognizing other artists and poets in my own creative work.

"As a writer, I return again to themes gleaned from my love of fine art, visual artists, and sensitive and brilliant writers whom I admire. This is a loving tribute to the warmth and intelligence of Alice Jane-Marie Massa."

[60] **The Queen's Staff.** Susan Lavender writes, "HRH Prince Philip, Duke of Edinburgh, died on 9th April 2021. He had been consort to Queen Elizabeth II of Great Britain and Northern Ireland for sixty-nine years, making him the longest-serving British royal consort to the longest-reigning current monarch. He had been the Queen's husband of seventy-three years. When Elizabeth became Queen regnant, upon the death of her father, King George VI, in 1952, Prince Philip gave up his very promising naval career to devote himself entirely to his new role as Queen's Consort. As he put it: 'My job first, second and last is never to let the Queen down.'

"In fulfilling her role as the cornerstone and anchor of the British constitutional system of government for over half a century, the Queen relied on Prince Philip's support and counsel. He was her 'strength and stay'. Her constant companion, he always accompanied her, walking two steps behind her in accordance with royal protocol. He always 'had her back'. He sat beside her at formal engagements and was at her side her throughout their life together.

"At Prince Philip's funeral on 17 April 2021, Queen Elizabeth walked and sat alone for the first time. She hesitated as she entered St. George's Chapel, Windsor, and seemed to look back for an instant. Inside the chapel she sat by herself, with no one next to her and wearing a mask, in accordance with Covid 19 pandemic requirements, but I believe Prince Philip was with her in spirit and always will be as she continues to carry out her duty, in her usual exemplary fashion, to the end.

"To mark what would have been Prince Philip's 100th birthday on 10 June 2021 the Royal Horticultural Society presented the Queen with a rose named after him which was planted in the garden of Windsor Castle."

[61] **At a Loss During the Time of Corona.** Birgit Bunzel Linder writes, "I wrote this poem for a poetry event entitled 'Human versus Virus'. The topic had been set early in the pandemic and was still politically charged. Although I am fond of writing poems about nature and animals, I had never considered writing about a 'virus', and at the time, we were still very much in the thick of this new and mysterious health crisis. I made several attempts to write something for the event until it occurred to me that being in the thick of it was exactly the problem: every single day something new happened, and we were constantly faced with an overload of information, much of it contradictory. Even the scientific discourses seemed inconsistent and at times even conflicting, and it left us with more questions than answers.

"One of the defining moments for the idea of this poem was a short video my sister-in-law sent me from Berlin: when the area in Kreuzberg was under lockdown, herds of wild pigs suddenly began to roam the streets, and they roamed exactly in those places that had previously been their forest habitats. Suddenly, stories like this appeared everywhere, animals literally coming out of the woods. It gave me the feeling that there is so much going on in this world that we are blind to. On the one hand, it was interesting to see how other creatures coped, and on the other, it was alarming to once again realize that nature pays the price for our lifestyles. The most authentic feeling I had (and still have) was being at a loss. It was such a wake-up call for humanity! I did feel that there was one big hope, though: that a crisis like this could perhaps change us for better; that we would ask important questions about life and ecology again; and that we would see the urgency to be better stewards of this earth. Faced with so many confusing thoughts, I decided to simply write about my own perplexity, and about all the new questions the Covid crisis posed for me."

[62] **Virus.** J. P. Linstroth writes, "The poem, 'Virus' was written in five parts. It was inspired by the spread of the COVID-19 (Coronavirus) pandemic throughout the world. The first part of the poem was inspired by the effects of Coronavirus in India and all of the thousands of cremations in places like New Delhi. The second part of the poem was inspired by the

collapse of the health care system in Manaus, Brazil and all the burials in the Taruma cemetery there. While the third part of the poem was inspired by disaster from the Coronavirus in Guayaquil, Ecuador where the dead were just left on the streets to be taken away at some future time. The fourth part of the poem was inspired by the happenings in a typical "intensive care unit" (ICU) at a hospital and the typical care for COVID-19 patients. And lastly, the fifth part of the poem was inspired by my own personal experience after having contracted the Coronavirus and what it felt like."

Note: "Saudades de vocês, saudades, muitos saudades": Spanish for, "Missing all of you, missing you, missing you very much."

[63] **Chia Pet.** Iris Litt explains "It's an adult toy cartooned as a human head with seeded grass that grows like hair when you water it. If you water it enough it will flourish just like the earth will. So it's a lesson in evolution."

As for a backstory, she writes, "I haven't much to say about it. It is a simple message, comparing our planet to a chia pet. A way to get people to deal with the size of the problem. A way to keep them from downplaying the size of it."

[64] **How to Forge a Heart.** Sharon E. Ludan writes, "Everyone experiences pain at some point in his/her life. It is part of the human condition. If we accept the pain, reflect on its possible causes, effects, and remedies, the experience may make us stronger and better prepared for life's challenges."

[65] **Seeking a Theory of Everything.** Sharon E. Ludan writes, "According to Wikipedia, 'A theory of everything is a hypothetical, singular, all-encompassing, coherent theoretical framework of physics that explains and links together all physical aspects of the universe... The theory of everything is a single theory that, in principle, is capable of describing all phenomena in the universe.'

"I, too, am seeking a theory of everything that reveals and explains the meaning of the universe."

[66] **An Infant's Prologue.** Wayne Paul Mattingly writes, "This poem was initially inspired by Loudon Wainwright III's song titled 'Dilated to Meet You.' It roused feelings about returning to the beginning (the womb) while being thrust out onto the world stage of Life. One can't go back or home or offstage until one's hour upon it is done."

[67] **Out of the Shoebox.** Wayne Paul Mattingly writes, "One of the remarkable aspects of seizure is returning – to consciousness – to life. This poem reflects that experience. The miniscule creature addressed *is as the speaker* – apparently. The need to identify with the creature identifying with the savior is paramount to survival. *Apparently.*"

[68] **My Indoor Cat.** Jack Mayer writes, "I am fascinated by the metaphysics of physics. 'My Indoor Cat' is a meditation inspired by my cat, Lucy. She tests, pokes, and prods her world in ways that remind me of how I do the same. Lucy and I, in our own ways, seek comfort by probing the unreachable and incomprehensible. I am fascinated by the mathematical theories we humans weave to explain the vast complexity of our universe. The interactions of quantum particles suggest the mysteries of relationships, of the contradictions between Newtonian and Quantum physics. I draw solace in camaraderie with Lucy as we try to decipher our particular place in our particular universe."

[69] **Vishvam.** Rianka Mohan writes, "I wrote this poem on Sunday, May 9, 2021. It didn't take me long – I say that not conceitedly because writing usually does, but because 'Vishvam' wasn't so much a poem that I wrote with my head; rather, an outpouring of feelings I held in my heart. India seemed to have Covid under control for a while – it was exporting the vaccinations it made – until the tide turned. Political rallies were held and in April, the *Khumb Mela*, the world's largest religious gathering with crowds so massive they can be seen from space, returned to our riverbanks. In the two months that followed, more than 300,000 souls paid the price for misplaced faith, while countless more waited to be mourned and to

matter. Six hundred children were orphaned over the summer. And that is the official count. I penned this on Mother's Day to celebrate, and cry for, who made me.

Notes:
Vishvam: word of Sanskrit origin meaning 'Universal'
Duryodhana: the main antagonist in the Hindu
epic, *Mahabharata*; a self-centred tyrant whose power-lust and desire for destruction of his rivals leads him to call for the Great War described in the book.
While it feels as if Covid-19 is like Duryodhana, politicians – ignoring health warnings – also seem to invoke his spirit.
Kurukshetra: The Great War of the *Mahabharatha* is to have taken place here. The *Khumb Mela* is held annually by the Ganges River.
adhan: The Islamic call to prayer.
Rudyard Kipling: English writer, born in India, which inspired much of his work.
Kabir Das: 15th-century Indian mystic poet and saint."

[70] **I Ask.** Gloria Monteiro writes, "Sometimes it seems that the question we threw in the ocean or on the mountaintop will one day come back with the answer and like a miracle will color the gray days our soul goes through.

"Sometimes we think all hope is in the answer to the questions we ask.

"Protection deprives us of freedom, of great laughter, of the tears of words, of the perfume of verses.

"To satisfy our desire to live long, we need to drink the divine word 'protection'.

"There are several shades of questions and various colors of protection and just a hint of flavor in the smile of mothers who, even without asking, are able to protect their children.

"In a sad look from my son, I asked in a poem, in a cloud, in the blood of a flower, if I am fulfilling my mission in this universe: 'If one day I will be able to protect you'.

"And it was only when I let go of all the tension that the word protection dragged on, did I fall into the arms of heaven.

"Perhaps gratitude will not bring a mother the answer, but it will always be the petals that receive and envelop my children.

"Protecting, in the culture of life of my characters, is dressing when it's cold, preventing us from falling in love if we can, letting the fingers of loved ones go in the wind, saving a piece of bread for tomorrow, rolling up our sleeves and getting milk to fill the bellies of our offspring and the heart of our beloved."

[71] **In the Waking Hours.** Natalie Nera writes, "As creative people we cannot and do not want to be shielded from the world around us, quite the opposite; our emotions, our ever-searching eyes, our ears that never stop listening reflect everything.

"The idea for the poem *In the Waking Hours* came from the stories I had heard over the past year and a half from my father who is a medical doctor. He is at retirement age, yet still works full-time. Moreover, in his spare time he also volunteers at the Covid ward. The powerful image of the medical workers helping their patients in incredibly difficult situations, the emotions, self-sacrifice, the loneliness of the last hour of a human life with a priest or a nurse but no family members... in that moment, I was all of those people and all those places of love, care and suffering, and the words just started pouring onto the page. That is how I got my first draft.

"I hope I managed to convey this amazing human ability to care, feel and act on compassion and protect the infirm and vulnerable."

[72] **The Day.** Philip Nourse writes, "The poem was written when I was twenty years old. I was at university in London at the time.I was going through an emotional period, with my mood swinging between moments of joy and deep melancholy. I wrote the words to reflect how I so often felt."

[73] **In Limbo.** Denise O'Hagan writes, "This poem was inspired by the long-term effects of grief (in this case, caused by my father's passing) and, less obviously, by my suspicion of the traditional 'linear' understanding of time. My father, a New

Zealander by birth, had spent a lifetime working abroad, mostly in Italy, and passed away just six months after his arrival in Sydney, where I had moved. He only knew his first grandson as a baby, and never met his second, and while the gap created by his absence seemed to grow rather than diminish as the years went by, so too did the sense my sons seemed to have of the person he had been. By being absent, his presence was, in a curious way, emphasised. I wrote this poem because poetry allows you to approach such a subject stealthily and obliquely and, in my opinion, illuminate the notion that the past never completely ceases to be."

[74] **[nameless].** Helena Oliver writes, "I happened to be in Tiruvannamali, India, at the time of the March 2019 mosque shootings in Christchurch (with 51 dead, including a three-year-old). With only patchy internet, I struggled to determine what had happened, let alone understand such a horrific senseless attack – until then, unimaginable in my country. I wrote this poem out of the shock and sadness I felt at that time. Our Prime Minister chose never to refer to the shooter by name, so that he should remain nameless."

[75] **dreamers and dust.** Helena Oliver writes, "This was written late 2018, after a visit to a provincial centre in outback Australia, six hours west of Sydney. I was struck by the aridity of the land, the many reminders of colonisation (stolid brick buildings, statues, street names) set in a wondrous purple haze of jacarandas in bloom – and the total absence of indigenous Australians or reference to their place in that land. Although still a year before the disastrous bushfires of the following summer, the futility of agriculture in such conditions was reinforced by the giant dust clouds I observed as with relief I set off to return home to Aotearoa New Zealand."

[76] **flowers grow from dirt.** Helen Oliver writes, "This poem was sparked by seeing this statement traced on the side of a dusty car. In my mind, it linked to the Buddhist image of the lotus flower emerging from polluted water – and the genesis of other things."

[77] **Reflections on Shoes.** Helen Oliver writes, "A poetry magazine had 'shoes' as the focus for its quarterly edition. This theme sparked the idea of the contrast between Gandhi and Imelda Marcos, as epitomised by their attitude to shoes, in their compassion for their people."

[78] **tossed in the tide.** Helen Oliver writes, "An avid beachcomber, I see many metaphors in the varied objects I find on the beaches of the Coromandel, New Zealand. This poem was sparked by a forlorn abandoned beach towel, twisted and sandy, yet surely able to be restored with a little effort ..."

[79] **Buried Alive.** Rena Ong writes, "This poem relates to the effort entailed in trying to bury emotions in order to avoid dealing with past mistakes, grief, regrets, anger and other strong emotions we are feeling for various reasons or when facing uncomfortable truths about ourselves. Yet at unexpected moments, these are recalled and we are transported and re-live the very things we have suppressed and are forced to confront once again. This causes us, as the poem alludes, to be so constrained we dare not go beyond our tidy house and garden and in fact build more boxes, as shown in the garden shed, to ensure we do not have to deal with them. Hence, we are buried alive."

[80] **Passing Days and Hidden Nights**. Jun Pan writes,
" 'Passing Days' and 'Hidden Nights' form a *montage* of time lapses. You may find similar experiences from the mini-stories depicted in the poems, many of which reflecting a coronavirus-influenced reality of life. The act(s) in a stanza can be considered a translation or interpretation of the time listed in each poem. In addition, the two poems constitute a duet, or a couplet, echoing each other in a unique sense. That's why time was recorded in different formats in these two poems."

[81] **At 3.06 On Saturday.** Peter Parle writes, "I am a supporter and season ticket holder of Liverpool Football Club, I wrote, 'At 3.06 On Saturday', approximately two weeks after the Hillsborough Disaster. At 3.06pm GMT on 15 April 1989 the Football Association Cup semi-final match between Liverpool

FC and Nottingham Forest was stopped due to a crowd surge after the matchday police opened a gate into the Hillsborough ground in Sheffield, where the tie was being played as a neutral ground to both teams. There was very little, if any, crowd control at that gate.

"The result of the surge led to the untimely deaths of 96 Liverpool supporters. A 97th name was added to the list on 28 July 2021 following the death of another victim of the disaster following the conclusion that his death was directly because of injuries sustained on the day.

"My main reason for the words I used was to ask angry questions as to why this happened after there had been very similar disasters occurred previously at football stadia. I also used the community unity that came from the disaster as the football rivalry between Liverpool and Everton supporters was forgotten as the whole City mourned the loss, terms like, '...an ocean of floral blue and red', and 'Linked Scarves across from Goodison....' Everton play in Blue at Goodison Park and Liverpool play in Red at Anfield stadium."

[82] **Christian's Beat.** Peter Parle writes, "During the European Football Tournament in June 2021, Denmark was playing Finland in a live televised game, when Christian Eriksen's heart stopped. He fell to the floor and was clinically dead. Paramedics and doctors were on the scene almost immediately and started CPR and set about with a defibrillator to bring him back from dead. His teammates formed a circle around him for privacy and discretion whilst the medics worked hard to save him. I put pen to paper the next day to capture what I had witnessed."

[83] **Farewell To A Princess.** Peter Parle writes, "The eponymous Princess is the late Princess Diana. The morning of my 41st birthday, I woke to the news that Princess Diana of Wales had died in a road traffic accident in a Paris tunnel. Her death not only affected the people of the UK, but it also had a massive impact across the globe. I was compelled almost immediately to write about her and how her life had touched so many people, and moreover how her death had touched so many more. Whilst there are many conspiracy theories about

how and why the Princess died the way she did, I wasn't paying any interest to those as I chose to write about her and the love people had for her."

[84] **Now!!!** Peter Parle tells us, " 'Now!!!', is a very personal piece of verse to me. My wife and I were married in the October of 1976. We were both very young and advised by many not to marry too young as it may not last due to life inexperience. We were relatively happy for the first five years and in December 1981 was the arrival of our Son. Consequently, my wife suffered from post-Natal depression, and weeks after our son was born her father died very suddenly. This, coupled with the depression put a strain on our relationship, despite my efforts to provide sufficient support, the stress took my Wife back to her sister's home whilst she tried to combat the issues that were affecting her ability to cope. I put pen to paper and expressed the best way I could that I wanted her back home and I needed to know that her love was as strong as mine. The words I chose to express myself in, 'Now'."

[85] **Confucius Temple In Qufu.** Joanna Radwańska-Williams writes, "While I was teaching at Nanjing University in the late 1990s, I went on a cultural tour of the UNESCO World Heritage Site of the Temple of Confucius and the tomb of Confucius in Qufu, in Shandong Province. This is one of the spiritual centres of China and of Confucianism, with over two thousand years of history. In the canopies of the beautiful tall trees in the courtyard of the temple, I was intrigued by the many egrets nesting there, oblivious to the flocks of tourists below. One of the tourist attractions at Qufu is to talk to living descendants of the clan of Confucius. I wondered whether the egret families had also lived in that place forever, in their parallel world of nature. This made me recall a documentary* I had seen about Heinrich Schliemann's discovery of ancient Troy. In the epic *Iliad*, in his enumeration of ships sailing to wage war on Troy from all over ancient Greece, the legendary poet Homer mentioned flocks of pigeons residing in the town of Thisbe in Boetia. When searching for the location of Troy, the archaeologists verified that flocks of pigeons still lived on

the site of the ruins of Thisbe even now, which lent credence to the accuracy of the details in Homer's geographical descriptions. In my associative memory, in my poem, the homing site of the flocks of pigeons became conflated with Troy (rather than Thisbe). These avian sentinels, whether egrets in China or wild pigeons in Greece, have lived in their own world of nature for many generations, unaware of the passage of thousands of years of human history in the civilizational centres of both East and West."

* *In Search of the Trojan War*, BBC series written and presented by Michael Wood, directed by Bill Lyons with Colin Adams as executive producer, broadcast in 1985. Review, "When Men Were Gods" by Edward Hudgins, accessed on 27th August 2021 at https://www.atlassociety.org/post/tv-review-when-men-were-gods .

[86] **In Praise Of Imperfection.** Joanna Radwańska-Williams writes, "This is a philosophical poem about the inherent imperfection of human beings. The middle stanza is autobiographical. When I was about nine years old, in London, I had a teacher who was mean to me. Perhaps, in her self-preoccupation with her own hurt, she genuinely did not realize that, as I was a fresh immigrant from Poland, my English was poor and I did not understand her teaching. Very soon, I came to regret my hatred for her, when I learnt that she had died of cancer. It was too late for reconciliation between us. And yet, in my deep regret, my hate turned to belated love, and after that in my life, I have never hated again."

[87] **My Polish Doll Lala Basia.** Joanna Radwańska-Williams writes, "This autobiographical poem was inspired by a poem about a plastic doll by Louisa Ternau, published in the 2019 edition of *Mingled Voices*. It has the same theme as Louisa's poem – the value of a plastic doll for a child. When I was growing up in the 1960s in Poland, I did not have a cornucopia of toys. The toys I did have were all very meaningful to me, in their artificial personages, in my make-believe childish world. They were almost like extra people in my family, especially my first doll, Basia. In Polish, 'lala' (also 'lalka') means 'doll',

while 'Basia' is the diminutive of the name 'Barbara'. My mother, Dr. Ewa Radwańska, who had lost her beloved doll Dziuba when her house was bombed and on fire in 1944 during World War II, lovingly brought me my second doll, Lucia/Bambina, from a conference trip to Italy in 1966. Unfortunately, none of these dolls remain with us now, only their memory. My mother has written about her doll Dziuba and my doll Lucia in her autobiography.*
*Ewa Radwańska, *Pomagając Kobietom i Matce Naturze: O moim życiu, medycynie, in vitro i nie tylko.* Warsaw, Poland: Dobry Skarbiec, 2018, pp19, 96."

[88] **After the Rain.** Coolimuttam Neelakandan Rajalakshmi (Raji) writes, " I had my thoughts gathered for my poem "After The Rain" after my stroll at many scenic spots in Hong Kong, especially during summer. The clear sky , freshness of the rain ,and the beauty of nature all adds to the soothing hope of what lies ahead."

[89] **Even then, in uncompromising winter.** M. Ann Reed writes, "As I watched Luke arrange a still-life arrangement, the *I-Ching* and its mitosis-meiosis mathematics came to mind, all to inspire this poem."

[90] **Incubating.** M. Ann Reed writes, "This poem records how my prayer, aligned with e. e. cummings's prayer, inspired my imagination and poem that practically 'wrote itself'. 'Temenos' refers to the safe-place provided for transformation. 'Bridget' refers to the saint, whom the Irish often regard as the bridge between heaven and earth"

[91] **When someone deeply loves you.** M. Ann Reed writes, "This poem aims to offer the epiphany experience of communicating with one of my dear friends who had recently passed. Overseas, I had missed his memorial service and had been mourning his loss to our community. This epiphany juxtaposes what had been my present scene, teaching for Nanjing Normal University IB World School in China with the past scene that my friend and I had shared in Portland, Oregon.

Dia de los Muertos is Spanish for Day of the Dead. 'Faraday Waves' are water waves that receive and transmit sound."

[92] **She who watches.** M Ann Reed explains as follows: "*She who watches* is the Native American name for a place overlooking the Columbia River Gorge. *Rain-flower stones* emerged from an ancient volcano near today's Nanjing, China. *Hua* in Mandarin refers to both language and flower. Just as the stones' language flowered from rain, so the people of Nanjing call themselves *the rain-flower stone people,* the people who also flowered from rain. Flowering language bridges Nanjing with Portland, often referred to as a people of rain, celebrating in the final paragraph a wise conversation overheard between a nine and eight-year old at summer camp."

[93] **Mother's Guilt.** Vinni Relwani writes, "Motherhood, with all its layers, runs a gamut of emotions and feelings. In sharing my thoughts and feelings with other mothers, and listening to them as they shared theirs, it was interesting, reassuring and even startling to find that one of the common themes was that of guilt, almost inherent in nature. This poem takes a zig-zag look at that, possibly intrinsic, connection."

[94] **Partition.** Vinni Relwani writes, "The story of the Partition, which created the separate countries, India and Pakistan, in 1947, was a traumatic one, and part of my family's history, making this story a personal one too. Strife and turmoil for the generations who experienced it firsthand. And for the generations that followed, a wake of questions. For those who were there, the pain of the event, and all it entailed, some of which was captured in this poem. For those of us who were born after the Partition, like myself, there's a feeling of loss of never knowing the homeland. And even deeper than that, thinking about the loss my parents and grandparents and their generation endured… and the heartbreak continues."

[95] **Vagrant Glances.** Dale Shank writes, "The poem's narrator, a foiled sleuth, is puzzled by experiences that change unpredictably. What he thinks he sees, may or may not be 'real.' I wrote the poem to portray visual phenomena as

metaphors for inexplicable, even contradictory, social perspectives where evidence and interpretation are dramatically different. How the brain processes images is better understood than how it processes ideas. Images travel from the primary visual cortex to other locations where first impressions are modified and stored. The narrator's dilemma might be caused by some 'neurological machination' that kicks in and extracts a long-ago-stored image which suddenly appears real to him. Who knows if ideas are subservient to similar machinations? I kept the poem ambiguous as to which, if any, images are 'real.' Reality is not an absolute."

[96] **Alchemy.** Hayley Ann Solomon writes, "This poem is essentially a love poem. I have crafted in cadence, a sprinkling of rhyme, a little iambic rhythm here and there, and the use of first person for immediacy. I move from the tentative to the trusting, from cold to warmth, and thus, metaphorically, from base metal to gold – alchemy."

[97] **Shadow-thought shielding.** Hayley Ann Solomon writes, "Psychological shields interest me. In this poem, I was exploring the concept of approaching distressing or disturbing thoughts peripherally, rather than confronting them head on.
As suggested in the poem, it takes bravery and tremendous strength of character to regard onself, one's follies, fancies, cruelties and errors head on.

"Most people don't, ignoring uncomfortable musings, or, more commonly, lying to themselves about motivation or outcomes.

"I look at an alternative to the outright lie - at a mechanism for confronting truth cautiously, mitigating pain and self contempt while at the same time allowing for insight and growth.

"The subject matter does not lend itself to the lyrical, hence no formal rhyme scheme, though I do use assonance and alliteration for stylistic integrity."

[98] **Silence, a shield.** Hayley Ann Solomon writes, "I am intrigued by the thematic concept of this competition. There are

so many ways to perceive shields beyond the more common, physical construct.

"In this poem I explore silence as a gift, a shield to protect the vulnerable – be it political or social.

"Sometimes blundering in, expressing sentiments of political or social sympathy and empathy can be counterproductive to the very people you wish to reach out to.

"Perhaps the greater gift, the one requiring more self restraint, is the one in which one says nothing. A case, possibly, of fools rush in where angels fear to tread. Choosing *not* to rush in, but to tread quietly, provides – possibly – a greater gift.

"In offering this backstory, I might be undermining the poem itself, a strange conundrum. Sometimes opacity is better than transparency."

99 The Girl with the Flaxen Hair. Abbie Johnson Taylor writes, "My father enjoyed playing the piano when I was growing up. He had no formal training but could read music, and I think he wanted to be like his brothers, who played the piano and guitar, and his father, who played the saxophone. My father played jazz standards pretty well after he practiced them. But he never fully mastered the one classical piece he took an interest in playing, Debussy's 'The Girl with the Flaxen Hair.' I was inspired to write my poem, 'The Girl with the Flaxen Hair,' after reading a similar poem by a fellow critique group participant about how his father played Debussy's 'Clair de Lune.' I found, on Wikipedia, the original poem on which 'The Girl with the Flaxen Hair' was based. I incorporated concepts from that poem to explain how my poor, dear father, may he rest in peace, inadvertently destroyed this beautiful creature with his attempt to play Debussy's work."

100 We, Flowers on Roadside Verges. Luisa Ternau writes, "The poem is centered on a duality between the wild flowers growing on the verges of roads and the mowers, where the latter stand for all that is evil and the former represent the beauty of life in its innocent form. The bees who cannot reach the flowers on time to collect their nectar evoke what is lost by not respecting the growth of such wild flowers. The only thinkable solution to escape the dreadful reality of this duel is to dream that the mowers would become inebriated with the smell of the flowers and then let go of their grip. The poem concludes with no clear view in sight as the freedom mentioned may just be temporary."

[101] **Sheltered in their Worlds**. Simon Tham writes, "It was early morning on 26 June 2021, when during sudden heavy downpour, the writer and the scholar met during their morning exercises in Kowloon Tsai Park. They had heard of each other's work previously through a mutual friend. As they sheltered under a dripping awning, they struck up a conversation and so learned more about each other. The writer was quite struck by the scholar's knowledge and was inspired to write this poem. He felt that their memories and experiences shelter them from the outside world."

Note: "Poeta Nascitur, non fit": Latin for "*A poet is born, not made*".

[102] **Ha Noi Alley**. Edward Tiesse writes, "Prior to visiting Viet Nam in 2014, I learned about families living in the alleys. So as not to violate their privacy, I tried to be as inconspicuous as possible when I wandered through the alleys and observed their lives. I discovered that these families were much like families around the world but their living rooms just happened in a public setting. I came to appreciate how normal their lives are with so little space."

[103] **Yellow Paint in My Blue Room**. Bibiana Tsang writes, "The poem was written as an attempt to organise fragments of thoughts in disarray. The colours yellow and blue are a reference to Van Gogh's letters and his many works, including the piece *The Bedroom*. Yellow is the colour of joy reiterated throughout the poem to counter the sombreness of the surrounding blue room. This work is dedicated to my friends, family and all who are suffering from emotional disorders and who are making the best out of what they have."

[104] **The Shielded World in Restaurants**. Roger Uren writes, "This poem is inspired by over five decades of experiences in restaurants, which have usually enabled my taste buds to enjoy food, but also provided a sense of relaxation or relief from personal or broader tensions and causes of concern. I have spent many years working as an Australian diplomat in Asia and America, and sometimes had to handle serious challenges. Dining in a restaurant, irrespective of whether it was a fancy or a simple environment, allowed one to distance oneself from the tensions and think coolly about possible solutions. Sometimes one also had personal problems, ranging from family issues to tensions with former friends, and while these could cause a lot of stress during the day a pleasant evening in a restaurant often helped me reduce the pressures that these problems could cause and enable me to relax. This poem is inspired by a sense of the positive role that restaurants can play that goes beyond just providing food and wine and shields one from depressing daily pressures."

[105] **It Had Begun Then....** Deepa Vanjani explains, "This poem was inspired by a scene in the film *Once Upon a Time in America*. Robert De Niro is so captivating, as usual, that I couldn't help writing this. The poignant pathos there was impelling. This is what happens when time has gone by and can't be turned around, no matter how much one wants this to happen."

[106] **Child**. Peter Verbica writes, "A university professor criticized me for writing without discipline. 'Child' is a poem in response to his chastisement; the poem is meant to be naked, impactful, and focused."

[107] **Feasting in Mexico**. Peter Verbica writes that this poem, "is arguably a non-fiction homage to the current poverty experienced in many small villages; while elitists fret over carbon footprints and climate change, the poor are bereft of such ponderings; they simply consume what they can to survive. This poem should not be mistaken as an appeal to some kind of Marxist utopia as might be trotted out by Marquez, Kahlo or Rivera. (A pragmatic and inglorious

certitude of property rights, as the learned Richard Pipes writes about with great insight, does more to ensure a population's welfare than any idealist's vision.) 'Feasting in Mexico' also takes on a greater ambit – not just how the mismanagement and corruption of a country's governance impacts the poor; it also cannibalizes a country's culture."

[108] **Secret Garden.** Peter Coe Verbica writes, "As the reader may intuit, the poem 'Secret Garden' is a nod to the actress and humanitarian, Audrey Hepburn. It imagines an ordinary protagonist so enchanted that he donates his fortune for a single dinner with the magnetic, self-effacing and introspective star."

[109] **The Runts**. Peter Coe Verbica writes that this poem, "is simply a push-back of today's 'cancel culture' keen on quieting the diversity of thought in their quest for power. Those who quell free speech are just demagogues dressed in colorful cloaks. They are not enlightened; they are merely goons who lambast all who dare to disagree with them."

[110] **This Snow**. Peter Coe Verbica writes, that this poem "is a critique of Eckhart Tolle (born 'Ulrich Leonard Tölle') and his wildly popular book, *The Power of Now*. Europe's moderns find it difficult to grow under the shade of an enormous tree – namely, their towering history. Modern art and architecture elbow out the nuance and craft of their predecessors with inhumane stark lines, cold surfaces and sharp angles. This poem attempts to speak to the quiet protests of a master engraver against anonymity; he embeds clues in many of his stamps: tributes to his friends, himself, his family. Today's youths, by and large, are no longer collectors of stamps and coins; such enchantments once helped generations have a strong sense of place, tradition and history. This poem also references other intriguing stamps from multiple countries; each stamp tells its own story – evidence not just of the 'power of now,' but also acknowledging the power of the past."

Asked to share further details, for example about the line, "The bulldogger painting of Ben instead of Bill", Peter Verbica further explains, "This poem is about a litany of stamp errors and also secrets embedded in stamps. The U.S. Postal

Service accidentally issued a stamp of the accomplished Black American cowboy Bill Pickett; the painter, Mark Hess, used a photograph which was incorrectly labeled and, in fact, was Bill's brother, Ben. The Pickett family notified the Postal Service after the issue, which quickly became valuable. The Postal Service then issued MORE of the stamps which were in error to prevent opportunists from capitalizing on the error; and the Postal Service also issued a corrected stamp which featured the actual likeness of Bill Pickett." Peter provides the following source for this information: https://postalmuseum.si.edu/exhibition/art-of-the-stamp-the-artwork-stamps-with-a-story/the-bill-pickett-incident

[111] **Eggs & Toast.** Kewayne Wadley writes, " 'Eggs & Toast' is essentially about a memory I had with a good friend. It explores the trapped feeling we face at one time or another with being an adult, with work compiled amongst other things. This theme really opens up about love and freedom. For example, 'Let's run away & pretend that we're kids' suggests that when I was with her, there were no other thoughts or worries and I could fully be myself when I was with her over a simple plate of breakfast, her name as well as her presence being that very same plate of breakfast that nourishes the mind, body, and spirit. After all breakfast is the most important meal of the day."

[112] **Freely.** Kewayne Wadley writes, " 'Freely' happens to be passion unbridled. With its quick burst of over a million ways to love your significant Lover. Very sultry and sensual, it takes an abstract approach to new-found worlds & the nuances of traveling through the dark, addressing all of the things that could go right or wrong. Surely love couldn't be one of those things that could go wrong. It uses a lot of metaphor to create the ambience that love is just as it is.

"Love. That rules or regulations shouldn't apply nor should it be stolen. In a world that sometimes embraces the cold. Love is the warmth that embraces. It is the heart and soul of every construct especially when discovering new-found worlds full of excitement and adventure."

[113] **Sunburnt.** Kewayne Wadley writes that 'Sunburnt' is, "Perfectly corky and offbeat. 'Sunburnt' is the comparison of a hot candle mixed with the heat of a relationship at its climax. With her being the ascension of flame. She burns bright and steadily consumes the wick without promise. Short and full of fire, 'Sunburnt' is sure to give new insights to candle watchers everywhere."

[114] **Shielding.** Victoria Walvis writes that, "'Shielding' is a found poem. The guidance on Covid 19 and ubiquitous information (and misinformation) can feel overwhelming, but I enjoy the way different words in different contexts seem to make accidental patterns. I started with an overwhelming amount of text from the internet and whittled it down to the phrases that seemed accidentally important. Phrases like 'people defined on medical grounds' seemed dystopian, while 'staying at home and having little guidance' seemed wryly cynical; but I also found the battle between the jargon and the human voices, in search of some sort of light, moving. Type 'Shielding' into Google and let your eye wander over the results. No doubt if I tried to write the same poem today, a very different one would emerge."

[115] **All the time.** Anson Wang writes, "This poem intends to unveil the complexity of love. Love is casual; love is causal. Love is the known unknown and the unknown known. It is a destined uncertainty."

[116] **On the way.** Anson Wang writes, "This is the second poem I wrote about my experience with the public transportation in Hong Kong. The poem consists of three periods, namely, morning, afternoon and evening. And this very short route of the minibus is a miniature of life. When the minibus takes me from home to work, it also takes me through important issues one may face in life, sickness and education. The poem also depicts different types of persons and their roles in life in a simple way, mini-bus driver, domestic helper, patients and their relatives or friends."

[117] **An Improbable Ruin**. George Watt writes, "A Google search for 'abandoned theme parks' reveals an astonishing number of them in various stages of decay around the world. They can be sinister, depressing, alarming, or arresting and amusing – even comic – in turn. My Google search was part of trying to rediscover the actual location of one such park, etched into my memory. I was on a long-haul flight but can't remember the airline or the route. Bored, half asleep, in desperation I reached, as one does, for the airline magazine and mindlessly flipped through it. But one article grabbed my attention. A photojournalist had captured what was left of one such theme park in the middle of a tropical jungle. What made this one singularly unusual was its distance from the nearest urban area or good roads or means of transport. It was literally in the middle of nowhere. One major gnarled and twisted structure still filled what used to be a cleared area. It was obvious that in a few years the fecund plant life would completely cover the fallen remains. It was one 20th Century equivalent of 'Ozymandias' though a jungle was doing the reclaiming, not the desert. Try as I might, I have been unable to find any further reference to the actual site discovered while exhausted on the aircraft. There is always the possibility that I might simply have been dreaming."

[118] **Poor Oot [Pour Out]**. George Watt explains that the term refers to, "the Scottish ritual throwing of coins from a means of transport to gathering children as the bride and father leave for the wedding, or other close family members. The *Scottish National Dictionary* cites J.H.A. MacDonald lamenting the passing of the custom in 1840s Edinburgh, but later references show that the custom continued, such as an article in the *Scottish Daily Mail* (25 July 1959) which describes the bride as laughing 'as her architect-trained husband leaned from the bridal car for the "poor oot" – the old Scots custom of throwing coppers and silver for children lining the pavement.' I also recall the custom being alive and well in the 1950s, both as a would-be participant in the street (which wasn't allowed) and from within the rare luxury of a large Austin Princess on the way to an aunt's wedding. 'Poor oot!' was the corporate cry of those waiting for the scramble for coins."

George Watt also tells us that, "The Glasgow Poems" are an as yet unpublished work in progress.

[119] **the music has seen to it.** George Watt writes, "I walk every day in a beautiful riverside park lined with massive eucalypts that belie the inner-city location of the suburb. It includes meandering paths, a bucolic cricket oval, a well-preserved billabong, home of various water birds – Grebes, Water Hens, various ducks, Sacred Ibis, a lone Pelican and a pair of Black Swans all three of which return to feed during the winter months. In the park there are various facilities for recreation, including public barbeques where families often gather. On a particular day a large and handsome dark-haired group from an Eastern European or Caucasian culture (I think, though I could not recognize their language) sang and danced to highly addictive music. I waved as I walked past, and they waved back. It was a memorable moment. Now when I pass that location, I cannot see it without their presence and hear their music. Every time I'm there I see them in my mind, hear their song, and return their friendly wave. They are always there in spirit, but only I have the eyes to see them. What's most important in all of this is that I have no choice but to do so. I'm intrigued by the idea that once *something* is seen *somewhere* (especially when music is around) that location is always inhabited by both. This is what I am trying to capture in "the music has seen to it". In the first incident in the poem a stagehand mistakenly came on stage after noisily crashing through double doors during a piano recital of Ravel's music. No matter where I am or what I'm doing: when Ravel is on the radio, or coming through Spotify, I can't help by see the look of shock on his reddening face when he realizes where he is. The pianist didn't notice him or pretended not to."

[120] **Treacle Toffee and the Grammar of Self.** George Watt writes, "I have always been interested in the ways that grammar helps organize and order our writing, our thought processes, and – more importantly – our place in the world and our sense of self. In an article about unique aspects of minority languages in India, Anvita Abbi in *Qrius* (8 September 2016) demonstrates that we miss much if we merely think of

grammar as a description of language structure and its components. It "encodes the thoughts, culture, attitudes, world-view, and identity of the speaker." In other words, you can only think of yourself in linguistic terms that you have at hand and that differing linguistic traditions will produce different selves. This poem tries to capture one or two of the psycho-linguistic complexities in Abbi's intriguing ideas. I set the poem in the childhood classroom for it is there that our idea of subject, object, self and other are foundationally established, both for good and ill."

As mentioned above, George Watt also tells us that, "The Glasgow Poems" are an as yet unpublished work in progress.

[121] **Winter Camp**. Michael Witts writes, "This poem is consciously written in the unadorned style of Constantine Cavafy, or at least the style of the English translations of his work. Like much of his work, this poem is not fixed in time or place. It is my inadequate response to the refugee crisis unfolding across the world as millions of persons are displaced by war and oppression. In early 2020 I took my Australian family on a trip to Europe to culminate in a snowboarding trip to Austria. As we crossed warm and snug in our bus from Switzerland to Austria we glimpsed what I took to be a refugee camp located on the border. This was my jumping off point to question what I was observing from the comfort of my own privilege and security. I am humble enough to know I have no answers."

[122] **To the Knees.** Fei Zuo writes, "Recently most of my poems are long.... But this poem is a short one, which meant I had to work harder on it. There were many things I wanted to say, but in what way? This concerned me the most.

"For me a short poem, especially the end of it, should be as powerful as a good short story. If begging to be touched by one's love (as shown at the end of the poem) should be the theme, it was like a secret I'd like to keep as long as possible until unraveled. With that in mind, I thought of all the possible narratives I'd known about knees before I'd go for that touchstone: to reveal the secret.

"As modern people, we read books, hear stories, and watch shows. These are all narratives, I mean, resources buried in our memory lanes, waiting to be stirred, or woven into lines of poetry. I once watched a show where a migrant worker comes to a family, asking for food and water, and a short stay. Somehow, the wife of the family, unlike her friendly husband, frowns at the vagabond. And this vagabond, before he leaves, puts a sign, a cross, on their door.

"This small detail was haunting. I remember I trembled as I saw this episode, for it reminded me of putting a signal on the doors in the Bible. Of course there are differences, for example, in the show the family, especially the wife, will probably be punished, whereas in the biblical allusion, a sign is made so that a certain person could be spared by God.

"This story of a roaming man might have overlapped with another piece in my mind: the life story of Georgia O Keeffe: a man looking for odd jobs walked into her ranch, and later became her lover and partner. But a roaming man might also end up becoming a captive. In *A Handful of Dust*, a novel by Evelyn Waugh, a man sets out for his adventures in the Amazon, only to be enslaved, forced to read Dickens indefinitely for an illiterate local man of power. And in a certain show I watched, a migrant young man is targeted as a love prey and then killed by a priest who offers him a shelter.

"Yes, the subject is knees, but the knees of a loved one are very hard to describe, simply because the border between love and hate is paper-thin, and the definition is almost beyond definition as it pushes boundary after boundary, especially when it comes to emotions not just for lovers, but also for parents and children, citizens and rulers. All in all, life is about dignity and shame. Whether to kneel down or not, literally or figuratively, seems to be decisive for many of us.

"So for me it is natural to imagine a man who's either an angel (an old angel though) or who will always remain young and beautiful, hopefully to be less subjected to a difficult life. Both actually can be characters in the stories of Gabriel Garcia Marquez. It is, however, hard to imagine whether they'd be able to enjoy ecstasy equally with humans, if they wouldn't also suffer the same pains as humans do."

SOME POETRY AND POETRY COLLECTIONS
Published by Proverse Hong Kong

A Gateway Has Opened, by Liam Blackford. 2021.

Alphabet, by Andrew S. Guthrie. 2015.

Astra and Sebastian, by L.W. Illsley. 2011.

Black Holes Within Us (translation from Macedonian),
by Marta Markoska. 2021

Bliss of Bewilderment, by Birgit Bunzel Linder. 2017.

The Burning Lake, by Jonathan Locke Hart. 2016.

Celestial Promise, by Hayley Ann Solomon. 2017.

Chasing light, by Patricia Glinton Meicholas. 2013.

China suite and other poems, by Gillian Bickley. 2009.

Epochal Reckonings, by J.P. Linstroth. 2020.

For the record and other poems of Hong Kong,
by Gillian Bickley. 2003.

Frida Kahlo's cry and other poems, by Laura Solomon. 2015.

Grandfather's Robin, by Gillian Bickley. 2020.

Heart to Heart: Poems, by Patty Ho. 2010.

H/ERO/T/IC BOOK (translation from Macedonian),
by Marta Markoska. 2020.

Home, away, elsewhere, by Vaughan Rapatahana. 2011.

Hong Kong Growing Pains, by Jon Ng. 2020.

Immortelle and bhandaaraa poems,
by Lelawattee Manoo-Rahming. 2011.

In vitro, by Laura Solomon. 2nd ed. 2014.

Irreverent poems for pretentious people,
by Henrik Hoeg. 2016.

The layers between (essays and poems), by Celia Claase. 2015.

Of leaves & ashes, by Patty Ho. 2016.

Life Lines, by Shahilla Shariff. 2011.

Moving house and other poems from Hong Kong,
by Gillian Bickley. 2005.

Over the Years: Selected Collected Poems, 1972-2015,
by Gillian Bickley. 2017.

Painting the borrowed house: poems, by Kate Rogers. 2008.

Perceptions, by Gillian Bickley. 2012.

Please Stand Back from the Platform Door,
by Vishal Nanda. 2021.

Poems from the Wilderness, by Jack Mayer. 2020.

Rain on the pacific coast, by Elbert Siu Ping Lee. 2013.

refrain, by Jason S. Polley. 2010.

Savage Charm, by Ahmed Elbeshlawy. 2019.

Shadow play, by James Norcliffe. 2012.

Shadows in deferment, by Birgit Bunzel Linder. 2013.

Shifting sands, by Deepa Vanjani. 2016.

Sightings: a collection of poetry, with an essay,
'Communicating Poems', by Gillian Bickley. 2007.

Smoked pearl: poems of Hong Kong and beyond,
by Akin Jeje (Akinsola Olufemi Jeje). 2010.

Of symbols misused, by Mary-Jane Newton. 2011.

The Hummingbird Sometimes Flies Backwards,
by D.J. Hamilton. 2019.

The Year of the Apparitions, by José Manuel Sevilla. 2020.

Uncharted Waters, by Paola Caronni, 2021.

Unlocking, by Mary-Jane Newton. March 2014.

Violet, by Carolina Ilica. March 2019.

Wonder, lust & itchy feet, by Sally Dellow. 2011.

POETRY ANTHOLOGIES
Published by Proverse Hong Kong

Mingled voices: the international Proverse Poetry Prize anthology 2016, edited by Gillian and Verner Bickley. 2017.

Mingled voices 2: the international Proverse Poetry Prize anthology 2017, edited by Gillian and Verner Bickley. 2018.

Mingled voices 3: the international Proverse Poetry Prize anthology 2018, edited by Gillian and Verner Bickley. 2019.

Mingled voices 4: the international Proverse Poetry Prize anthology 2019, edited by Gillian and Verner Bickley. 2020.

Mingled voices 5: the international Proverse Poetry Prize anthology 2020, edited by Gillian and Verner Bickley. 2021.

Mingled voices 6: the international Proverse Poetry Prize anthology 2021, edited by Gillian and Verner Bickley. 2022.

FIND OUT MORE ABOUT PROVERSE AUTHORS, BOOKS, EVENTS AND LITERARY PRIZES

Web: <http://www.proversepublishing.com>
Our distributor's website:
<https://cup.cuhk.edu.hk/Proversehk>
twitter.com/Proversebooks
www.facebook.com/ProversePress

Request our free E-Newsletter
Send your request to info@proversepublishing.com.

Availability
Available in Hong Kong and world-wide
from our Hong Kong based distributor,
the Chinese University of Hong Kong Press,
The Chinese University of Hong Kong, Shatin, NT,
Hong Kong SAR, China.
See the Proverse page on the CUHKP website:
<https://cup.cuhk.edu.hk/Proversehk>

All titles are available from Proverse Hong Kong,
http://www.proversepublishing.com

Most titles can be ordered online from amazon
(various countries).

Stock-holding retailers
Hong Kong (CUHKP, Bookazine)
England (Ivybridge Bookshop)
Canada (Elizabeth Campbell Books)
Andorra (Llibreria La Puça, La Llibreria).

Also, orders may be made from bookshops
in the UK and elsewhere.

Ebooks
Most of our titles are available also as Ebooks.

Made in the USA
Middletown, DE
25 March 2022

63156990R00166